SPORTSMAN'S BEST

BOOK & DVD SERIES

FS Books:
Sport Fish of Florida
Sport Fish of the Gulf of Mexico
Sport Fish of the Atlantic
Sport Fish of Fresh Water
Sport Fish of the Pacific

Baits, Rigs & Tackle
Sportsman's Best: Sailfish
Sportsman's Best: Redfish
Sportsman's Best: Inshore Fishing
Sportsman's Best: Snapper & Grouper
Sportsman's Best: Offshore
Annual Fishing Planner
The Angler's Cookbook

Florida Sportsman Magazine
Shallow Water Angler Magazine
Florida Sportsman Fishing Charts
Lawsticks
Law Boatstickers

Author, Mike Holliday
Edited by Joe Richard and Florida Sportsman Staff
Art Director, Drew Wickstrom
Illustrations by Joe Suroviec
Copy Edited by Jerry McBride

www.floridasportsman.com

INSHORE FISHING

CONTENTS

SPORTSMAN'S BEST
INSHORE FISHING

56

142

Inshore fishing has numerous appeals. Calmer conditions on most days compared with offshore, less fuel expense, shorter hours, more time to reflect.

Welcome to Inshore Fishing

More anglers than ever are discovering the excitement of inshore saltwater fishing.

Whether approaching the seashore from inland or backing off from the ocean depths, record numbers of fishermen find themselves hooked solid by the powerful allure of close-in coastal action.

We're into it for many reasons, one of which may simply be that your next trophy catch is swimming relatively close to home, rather than a half-day, roller-coaster, bluewater boat ride away.

Maybe you enjoy the high-energy environment where land meets sea at the foamy beach, or that wave-swept jetty or raging inlet. Or perhaps you go for something more tame, such as a flooding, gin-clear tidal flat, a spartina-lined marsh creek, a winding estuarine river, or a remote backcountry bay. Hey, whatever style of fishing floats your inshore boat, it awaits you 12 months a year, somewhere along the coast from Texas clear to the Northeastern U.S.

Though you may choose to specialize, limiting your fishing to one species with one fishing method, most inshore enthusiasts enjoy the wide variety of inshore gamesters that abound, thanks to a growing conservation ethic among avid inshore anglers. It's said that variety is the spice of life, and inshore salt-water fishing delivers it big time.

Best yet, there is a commonality among inshore fisheries from state to state. Your tackle and tactics that catch flats redfish in Florida will catch 'em in Texas, Louisiana, and the Carolinas, too. Fish your favorite trout plug in striper country, and you had better hang on! And it's not surprising that bass anglers are coming aboard in droves, because in many cases, their style of fishing works well on inshore salt waters. That just touches upon perfect examples of cross applications that tie Gulf and Atlantic inshore fisheries together, and broaden the inshore game's appeal.

And that's the message that the editors and writers of *Shallow Water Angler* and *Florida Sportsman* magazines bring to you in issue after action-packed issue, and now, in the only saltwater inshore fishing book you'll likely ever need, *Sportsman's Best: Inshore Fishing.*

Read on, and we'll see you on the water!

Mike Conner

Editor, Shallow Water Angler Magazine

Inshore fishing may be close to shore, but you never really know what the next cast will produce. How about that 100-pound tarpon you've always dreamed of catching?

Everything You Need to Succeed

From school-sized seatrout to giant tarpon, you never really know what that next cast will produce. That's the attraction of inshore fishing. Every cast provides the chance to produce a strike that will bend your rod like a banana, or make your reel scream for mercy.

Knowledge is a major component of fishing success. This book will not only direct you to the fish, but show you the little nuances that increase your catch rate. From picking the right tackle to the best baits, you'll find all the information you need here to consistently catch fish along the coast.

As a bonus the hosts of *Shallow Water Angler* and *Florida Sportsman TV* have produced and included a 60-plus minute DVD that follows the book with instructional and entertaining video footage.

So take advantage of the knowledge and expertise of the editors of *Florida Sportsman* and *Shallow Water Angler* magazines.

My father took me fishing for the first time when I was seven years old. Using spin gear and live shrimp, we tried for mangrove snapper in a South Florida canal. The various fish we caught that day were not exceptional, but I was amazed at the variety. A big impression. The kid was hooked.

Although the Sunshine State is still home, I've had the opportunity as an outdoor writer to fish much of the coastal United States. It's the greatest job in the world, and not a day goes by that I don't appreciate that good fortune. Doing what you love for a living doesn't come without sacrifice.

My mother would describe me in high school as a good kid, but entirely too consumed by fishing. "Fish, fish, fish," she would say. "All you do is fish. You're never going to amount to anything if you do that."

Well, I still fish a lot, but now with my children. I still have the same passion for the sport, and make a living. You could say fishing has enriched my life in many ways. I think Mom would be proud. Now my job is to help hook a new generation of seven-year olds, and their kin. Let's catch 'em.

Author, Mike Holliday

CHAPTER 1

The Appeal of Fishing
Inshore Waters

From Maine to Texas, this country has some of the most beautiful waterways in the world. Even more impressive are the numbers and varieties of fish that live in those waters. If you like light tackle or fly fishing, you'll quickly learn to love inshore fishing.

Each state has something different to offer, from rocky shorelines that dip down from the cliffs onto the beach to expansive marshes and wide open bays. Each area is unique in it's offerings, and it's up to you to learn the little nuances that will make these special fishing areas into your favorite memories.

Inshore fishing is as much a communal with nature as it is an effort to outthink the fish. Even in a downtown urban setting, most anglers can find some peace and solace in casting a lure or bait along the shore of a bridge or seawall. If the beauty of the location doesn't capture your heart, then the challenge of fooling the fish will. No matter where you travel along the coastal United States, there's a fantastic fishery waiting for your attention. It may be in your back yard or hundreds of miles away from home, but just give it a little bit of your free time, and it will touch your soul forever.

Ever wonder why so many anglers have turned to inshore fishing? Read on.

Inshore fishing often means casting in sheltered waters. That's a welcome respite for many anglers who have previously sampled offshore fishing.

The World of Inshore Fishing

Welcome to the world of inshore saltwater fishing, the fastest growing segment in sport fishing today. Whether you're a seasoned veteran or a novice angler wanting to learn about how, when and where to fish in your coastal waters, this book will teach you about the fish and the fishing techniques that make this sport so exciting—while providing a solid base of inshore fishing knowledge.

Inshore fishing is for anyone. Maybe you've honed your casting skills on trout streams and bass lakes, or trolled the deep blue for billfish and tuna. There's no doubt, then, that you'll recognize certain elements of inshore fishing. With minor adjustments in tackle and strategy, you'll soon find new rewards on coastal bays, brackish deltas and tropical grassflats.

The only requirement for success is a willingness to learn and a passion for being on the water. Be careful, because it won't take long for the fishing bug to bite; once it does, you'll find there's a world of opportunity around every turn of the coastline. Suddenly, you'll find yourself looking at water and wondering what fish live below and how you can catch them. It's this new appreciation for inshore fish that will make you want to try new tactics and techniques and master the challenge of catching different species of fish.

For many anglers, fishing becomes a significant part of their everyday lives, one that provides relaxation, recreation, sport and sometimes even food for the table. These anglers take their fishing seriously, and strive to gather as much fishing know-how as possible through books, magazines, television, seminars and word-of-mouth.

Ultimately there's no substitute for time spent on the water. However, the original base of fishing skills must come from somewhere, and that's where this book comes into play. As we walk you through each chapter of the world of shallow-water angling, you'll

Desperate battle in close quarters: flyrod-hooked fish fights to reach protective cover.

Big fish lurk in sheltered bay waters. This 16-pound snook blasted a plug fished near mangrove trees.

gain the knowledge to improve your understanding of fish and inshore fishing. Wherever you hit the water, the information you retain from this book will make it easier for you to choose the right gear and techniques to catch more inshore gamefish.

The editors of *Florida Sportsman* magazine have been teaching anglers about fishing

Florida waters for over 35 years. Their newer *Shallow Water Angler* magazine covers the inshore scene from Texas to New England. One would be hard-pressed to find a better source of fishing expertise and photography. More important than their credentials is their passion for fishing and teaching others about the sport. At least two generations have been

Predator and Prey

There's more to fishing than just catching fish, and that's certainly true on inshore waters. You will have the opportunity to explore different marine habitats and learn more about fish and other creatures that share these areas. Eagles, herons, sea turtles, alligators and porpoises will be your constant companions. For many anglers, this is where they learn appreciation for the great outdoors—and the reality of predator and prey relationships. This is where anglers gain an inner peace from just being on the water and interacting with a wide variety of coastal wildlife.

Inshore fishing can be therapeutic as a means of relaxation and a time for contemplation—an opportunity to silently work out life's challenges, while concentrating on the next cast. Here your mind is free to drift as you explore new waters. SB brought up fishing in Florida with FS magazine. As the old saying goes, "Bring a kid a fish, and you feed him for a day. Teach a kid to fish, and you feed him for a lifetime." Or something like that.

As a child I was bitten by the fishing bug, a common affliction with virtually all FS and SWA writers and editors. My father took me

inshore fishing for the first time when I was seven years old, and although we only caught a few small mangrove snappers, those fish represented an entire new world of life below the water's surface. By the time I turned 10, I would leave my house every summer morning with a fishing rod in hand. My mother would give me a couple of dollars to cover the cost of

Predators above and below the water prowl for food on a daily basis.

Glory moments: shallow-water redfish above was fought and landed on the quiet flats. Below, a hooked tarpon flies from the water during a sunset bite.

bait, tackle, lunch and a few sodas, and I'd pedal away on a bicycle, knowing I had to be home for dinner at a certain time.

I used treble hooks to snag mullet, and then let the baitfish swim around the canals of South Florida with the hook still embedded. One day I had just snagged a mullet and was reeling it in when the largest fish I'd ever seen ate that bait right at my feet. I'd heard stories of tarpon, but had never seen one in real life. Every inch of line tore off my reel, as the fish jumped its way up the canal. Spooled!

A dozen years later I returned to that very same canal and caught my first tarpon on a fly rod. It was a milestone I'd been seeking for several years. That fish was only a juvenile compared with bigger tarpon I'd encountered, but I'll always wonder if they were somehow related, if some innate bond with that first tarpon brought me back to a small canal in the middle of Miami to accomplish the feat.

I've caught hundreds of tarpon since, but those two fish remain etched in my memory like it happened yesterday. For you it might be a similar experience, the first fish that takes line or clears the water. Whatever works for you, touches your soul and makes you want to see and learn more about inshore waters, that's what counts. It's waiting there in all inshore waters.

And what are inshore waters? We'll define them generally as any body of salt or brackish water bordering or connected to the coast. Narrowing it down a bit, let's include only the first mile or two of ocean along the beach, and then all waters inland of that zone to the line—however gray—at which they mix with freshwater systems and the salinity level becomes too low to support saltwater marine life. Keep in mind that many of the best inshore fishing waters are brackish estuaries and coastal marshes that provide the perfect combination of food and

habitat to support immense marine fish populations.

Part of the fun of coastal fishing is the variety of fish that can be caught. You literally never know what the next cast will bring---a fish that barely teases the drag on the reel, or a leaping, fighting mass of fins, scales and swim-

It's a mixed-up world on the flats: above, redfish and black drum tail together. Below, a fine spotted seatrout caught wading.

ming fury. The trophy gamefish that will take every inch of line on your reel or test every skill in your repertoire is just a cast away.

Many of your fondest memories will be of days spent on the water, fish caught and lost, special moments with family and friends. Or while plying the waters alone, for that matter.

Every fishing trip is a new opportunity for results, but more importantly it's a chance to have fun. And escape the stress and noise that have become common in every day living. SB

CHAPTER 2

Assessing the Options

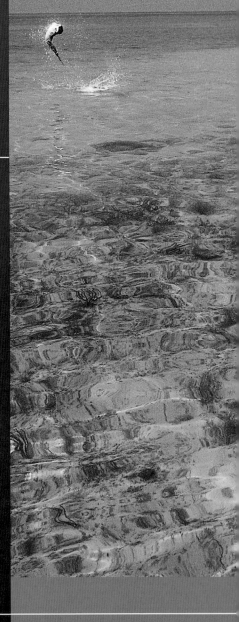

When you get to the point that you look at water and need to know what fish lie beneath the surface, you can consider yourself a true fisherman. As you experience the different facets of fishing such as trolling, drifting, blind casting, wading surf fishing, you'll likely gravitate to one type of fishing that just does it for you. It's not that the other styles don't have their appeal; in fact, many inshore anglers practice a variety of fishing techniques.

Whatever that technique, you will find yourself going at it with a passion. You'll develop the casting skills and knowledge base that improve your catch rate and exponentially increase the fun of inshore fishing. You'll find there are enough different casting and fishing techniques to dedicate a lifetime to mastering those skills. And what a lifetime of fun can would be!

Whether you're a serious angler or just like to wet a line now and then, the time spent learning fishing techniques will certainly be the basis of some great fishing memories.

Owning a boat has its magic moments, but you can always switch to wade, surf, bridge or pier fishing.

Classic gear and determined stance versus a classic fish: a big tarpon claws its way into the sky, hooked on a simple fly rod. Photo taken west of Key West in late May.

Getting Your Feet Wet

One of the most attractive aspects of inshore fishing is that you can do it with or without a boat. For many veteran anglers, deciding on a mode of approach is more than just a budgetary question. There are times when the most successful strategy is to get your feet wet.

WADERS CATCH THE BIG ONES

Wading is how many inshore anglers get started, and it's how many end up. This is the closest we will come to being a part of the marine world. Standing in the water, we are more likely to sense the environment around us. Down nearly at eye level with our quarry, we're more in tune with what they see, and with our feet in the water, touching bottom, we're certainly going to know more of what fish feel. This helps us understand what fish think, what attracts them to an area and why they feed there.

Wade fishermen shuffle along, getting a feel for shallow bottom that can't be analyzed effectively by looking or boating over it. When a wade fisherman's shoes sink into mud or bump against a rock or reef, he knows exactly what is at his feet. The same goes for shells, grass, sand holes or any bottom composition. Wading is like sitting in the front row of a classroom; you can't help but learn something.

Wading offers a complete understanding of bottom contours. Water getting deeper? You know it right away. Little dropoffs, sandbars and dips in bottom contour serve as ambush points for feeding gamefish. They're also comfort zones if the current increases or the weather turns sour. Either way, they're primary fishing spots.

Wading is easy on your time and your wallet. There are no trailers to hook up, no gas and oil tanks to fill, no tow vehicle or long ride to the boat

Trophy Hunters

Your slow and silent approach keeps most fish from detecting you. You can sneak in tight for short casts with lures and baits. Waders have noticed that trophy fish in thin water (spotted seatrout, for instance) can detect a drifting boat up to 60 yards away. You can see these fish leave the area, pushing a v-wake. Not so for quiet waders, who nail some huge trout. There's just no match for the low profile and silent approach that is intrinsic to wade fishing. SB

Wading a high tide in flooded spartina grass is a real kick for point-blank redfish action.

Trophy trout brought to hand in South Florida. This angler preferred to wade.

ramp. Just throw a few rods in the car and drive right to the spot.

BRIDGE AND PIER PEOPLE

Prefer to stay dry? Bridges, piers, jetties and sandy beaches offer lots of opportunity for shore-bound angling. On any given day, an angler is just as likely to catch a striped bass casting a big plug from a rocky outcropping as

he is trolling down the beach. There has been many a big snook caught by anglers fishing from Florida bridges.

When I was in my early 20's I didn't have a lot of money, but I could always jump in my car and drive to the nearest bridge. I spent many days and nights on the bridges of Southeast Florida, and I still fish them on a regular basis, though sometimes by boat. I

Bridge and pier anglers are legion and they catch their share of big fish, too. They just don't like to get their feet wet. That's a bay bridge at right, and a surf pier below. Both offer comraderie and good fishing at little or no cost.

learned valuable tactics for finding, hooking, fighting and landing fish, all while dangling bait over a railing or climbing down some ladder to fish a bridge fender.

SURF GUYS AND GALS

Surf fishermen in many states find great fishing with a four-wheel-drive vehicle, often during questionable weather that limits boating. The same high surf conditions or shifting winds and tides that make fishing from a boat a safety hazard can be a boon to surf anglers, who simply drive down the beach and pick a nice stretch of protected water inside the breakers.

Surf fishing also allows anglers to be more selective of their spots and to avoid the crowds, when they prefer to fish alone. There's just something special about having sand between your toes while battling gamefish. Whether you're standing waist-deep throwing jumbo swim plugs, or sitting on that tailgate or beach chair watching a long rod in a sand spike, it's the beauty, challenge and enjoyment that make this so much fun.

BOAT ANGLERS

There are popular areas for surf anglers, often near inlets or points that can draw a crowd, and for good reason. There are also remote locations that, although more difficult to access, certainly make the effort worth the rewards. At some point in every angler's life, the prospect of buying a boat becomes appealing.

Today's inshore fishermen can choose from a wider range of vessels than ever before. Best of all, we now have specialty boats and propulsion systems that afford access to waters previously considered unnavigable.

There are distinct advantages to fishing from a boat. The most significant is the ability to reach water that doesn't see a lot of fishing pressure. In many areas, development (or the

Bulls on the beach! This North Carolina angler drags a 40-pound redfish up a steep beach.

lack thereof) keeps anglers from reaching the fish. Those areas are like fish sanctuaries, where a lack of pressure creates opportunity. Fish may be more abundant and willing to feed. A classic example is the bonefish popula-

Covering Ground

Boats open up a world of fishing techniques not available to shore-bound anglers, and some of these techniques are extremely effective. Take trolling, for instance: Pulling a lure or bait with the boat allows you to target a certain depth and cover a lot of ground. That's important when trying to catch fish that are moving rapidly, or when you're unsure of where the fish are. Trolling is certainly best for rapidly moving, schooling gamefish like mackerels and bluefish.

Drift fishing is another great approach when fishing from a boat; it allows you to cover ground at a speed (depending on wind and tide) that lets you blanket the entire area with casts. Catch a few fish and you can throw a small marker buoy or record the position on a Global Positioning System (GPS) to focus on where the action is. Fishing a mile-long stretch in this manner requires little effort, other than casting and reeling. Unless you count unhooking fish. Imagine the effort expended to *wade* that far. SB

tion of The Bahamas. In the more developed areas where these fish get considerable pressure from waders and boats, these fish often travel in small schools that can be spooky and difficult to fool. Meanwhile, on the outer islands that are a long boat ride, bonefish mass in great schools that will literally swim up to the angler and fight over a jig, bait or fly. Even around boats.

Elevation can be something of an advantage. With the aid of a push pole or trolling motor, anglers aboard a flats skiff can creep along quietly, scanning the water to find fish. From the poling platform or elevated bow casting deck, it's possible to notice subtle details that may be obscured to wading anglers—like which direction a fish is facing. Some Texas shallow-water skiffs carry *three* separate casting towers.

A boat can also be a simple transport vehicle to a fishing spot not accessible from land, yet the kind of water where an angler might want to anchor up and get out and wade. The only function of the boat was angler transport. Without a boat, anglers would never get a shot at those fish. SB

Drifting is the most popular means of sneaking up on fish in a tidal creek. Opposite, other anglers pole their boat within casting range of shallow, visible fish.

See DVD for more on drift fishing.

Eyes locked on the prize, this angler lets fly at shallow water fish that are visibly within casting range.

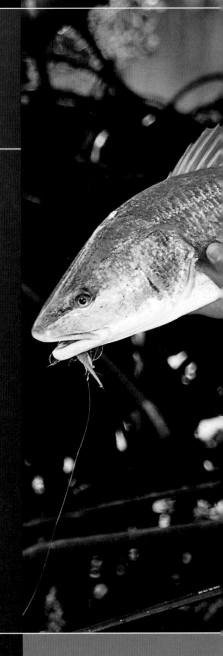

CHAPTER 3

Tackle Options:
The Basics

About every 10 years, fishing tackle improves by leaps and bounds, as gear becomes lighter, stronger and easier to master. Baitcasting reels (the old level-wind reels your dad or grandfather used) now have magnetic brakes to slow the spool and prevent the line from over-riding itself. (often called a "backlash" or "bird's nest"). Spinning reels now have multiple ball bearings in their moving parts, and synthetic gears to make them lighter and easier to use during a long day. Fly reels have large spools to pick up more line with each crank of the reel. They also sport cork and synthetic drags, and machined aluminum frames. In short, tackle keeps getting better as technology develops better materials and designs.

Think of your tackle much like a carpenter views his tools. Good tools make almost any task easier. The same holds true for fishing tackle.

Learn to match the right tackle for certain situations and fish. And ask yourself—are you after dinner, sport or both?

See DVD for more on inshore fishing tackle.

This angler just nailed one fine redfish on fairly light tackle. Notice he's using braided line for some hard pulling around the mangrove tree roots. Sometimes you have to pull extra hard around such heavy structure.

TACKLE OPTIONS:

Reels

O ne of the first decisions new anglers make is deciding which type of fishing reel fits best in the hand, and is easiest to work with. Most anglers begin with spin and then step up to bait-casting tackle. The appeal of spin-ning reels is no surprise---they're simple to operate, and don't back-lash like a baitcasting reel, so there's less skill required. Spin also throws far into a stiff wind without fear of backlash. With baitcasting gear, that's usually a dicey proposi-tion. The larger handles on spin reels also make them easier to turn quickly when trying to gain line on a fast-moving fish.

Spinning Reels

Spinning reels are the favored option when fishing with live bait-fish that aren't very aerodynamic, often hanging up in the wind. An errant cast into the wind with spin will result in a shorter than expected cast, but the same cast with baitcasting may result in an untimely backlash, as a school of fish approaches. (That may result in a cry of despair, depending on the angler.) If you're on the water and expect to be casting directly into the wind, spin is the obvious choice. If in doubt, carry both types of gear.

Most spinning reels these days are just upgraded versions of the first reels that came out in the 1960s and 70s. Back then, the reels were made of cast steel and were typically heavier and bulkier than reels seen today. There wasn't much graphite, aluminum or Teflon being used, if any, and yet the reels of yesteryear were surprisingly efficient. Simplicity of mate-

rials, with fewer moving parts and fewer things to break, is the reason some early-model reels are still around today.

Contemporary reels come with tremendous advantages. Less weight is a factor when cast-ing or fighting fish over long periods of time; you'll feel the difference in your wrist, hands and forearms.

One of the biggest breakthroughs in spin-ning tackle in the last two decades was the

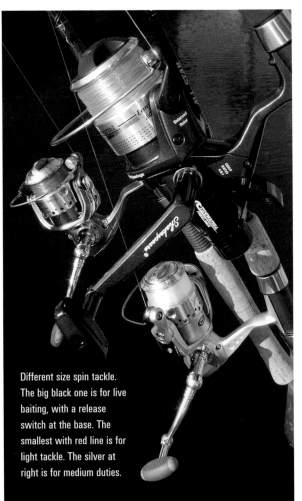

Different size spin tackle. The big black one is for live baiting, with a release switch at the base. The smallest with red line is for light tackle. The silver at right is for medium duties.

advent of taller, larger diameter spools that make for quicker retrieves. These taller spools also improve casting distance, as the line rolls off the spool in larger loops, causing less fric-tion off the reel. At one time, almost every reel company had spin reels with tall spools,

Variety of proven, inshore rods and reels with
different lines, designed for different situations,
casting ability and fish.

Lean into him!
The simplicity of
spin tackle makes
it a joy to use. Fish
fight harder on
spin, too.

marketed for longer casts. The drawback to these spools was decreased line capacity. Braided lines (which we'll look at later in this chapter) soon came to the rescue, so we still see a lot of reels with tall spools.

Nice spotted seatrout landed on spin tackle. This is ideal gear for long casts on open grass flats.

Drag systems— your "brakes" for slowing hard-running fish—have undergone a change, with some drags at the rear to make them easier to adjust when fighting fish, but most experts still prefer the traditional front-drag configuration.Different drag materials have added to the lightness in new reels, and many are made of synthetic materials that resist the normal wear and tear of big fish and salt water.

Quite a few fishing reels now have a series of ball bearings inside the gearbox to facilitate easy, consistent rotation around the spool. Reels with five, six or seven ball bearings tend to run smoother than those with fewer, but over time the wear factor on the gears seems consistent no matter how many bearings you have in the reel. Still, there's a comfort factor involved in using reels with numerous bearings; a reel with more bearings is preferable to one with fewer. Beware of bargain reels sold with the promise of many bearings: corrosion can eat up inferior components (ball bearings especially) in no time.

Bring a Spare

Many reel companies offer an extra spool with the reels they sell. This allows you to fill each spool with a different line. That means two different sizes, or a mix of monofilament and braided line. Use either lighter line for better casting distance, or stronger line when bigger fish appear. Also, and this is important, today's spin reels have handles that work on both sides. They take only a few seconds to adjust. Many people don't realize this, and end up reeling a spin outfit improperly, often with the reel upside down.

Baitcasting Reels

Baitcasting reels are another animal altogether. These reels have undergone similar changes in technology, just like their spin counterparts. Not long ago, the average baitcasting reel required a practiced, educated thumb to control a fast spool during the cast, to prevent a backlash. These days, many now carry adjustable magnetic brakes, that can be

Round baitcasting reel at bottom was a classic and standard for many years. More modern baitcasting reel at top has a more streamlined design.

able using baitcasting gear with certain plugs, that require a lot of action from the rod. The smaller reel handles (and cozy reel fitting into an angler's palm) allow for more action on the lure with simple wrist movements. For a long day of peppering timbered shorelines with accurate casts, baitcasting gear excels.

Line capacity is another improvement, something to consider when purchasing baitcasting reels. The smallest reels may be enjoyable to cast, but they offer limited line capacity. A big fish has to be stopped before it takes all the line, often by chasing on foot or by boat. For bigger fish, it's better to use a wide-body reel with greater line capacity. These bigger reels have bulked-up components to withstand the rigors of fighting big fish, and the pressure of testing the line's maximum breaking strength.

Add quick-release sideplates that let you get into the workings of the reel, interchangeable spools with different line capacities and even line counters, and you can see where technology has made using these reels a lot easier to use.

The thing to remember when purchasing a fishing reel is that no reel does it all. There are compromises to make. However, you'll likely accumulate more tackle as you expand your fishing experience. If you take good care of tackle, it will last for years and maybe an entire lifetime. How?

fine-tuned to create the perfect balance between long casts and line control. These brake systems make it much easier for rookie anglers to make long casts, and with more accuracy.

That accuracy is a key advantage to baitcasting reels. Many anglers are more comfort-

Clean Your Tackle

Keeping up with lubrication and cleaning will make them operate better and last a lot longer. After every use in salt water, reels should be cleaned by lightly spraying fresh water on them and then hand-wiping them dry. Spraying water with any force can push water and salt residue into the reel housing, or wash away lubricating grease or oil. The same can happen by dunking reels in a bucket of water, or using soap or cleaning products other than a lubricating oil to clean off the outside finish. After drying the reels, lubricate them lightly, and then check all the moving parts to make sure they're well oiled and in good working order. It may seem a tedious regimen, but it will greatly increase the overall life of each reel.

Cleaning a reel after every trip is important enough, but fishing around salt water requires a good rinse and frequent inspections.

Gear For All

Though not nearly as popular as baitcasting gear, there is also something to be said for the ease of using push-button, closed-faced reels. Here a six-year-old with a Scooby-Doo rod and reel outfit puts a whupping on fish. The casting and drag systems are simple but they work very well—as the sheepshead and seatrout on that particular day can attest.

TACKLE OPTIONS:
Rods

A rod influences casting distance and accuracy, and the amount of pressure you can put on a fish. Like reels, rods are built for both spin and baitcasting styles, with respective features that enhance the use of both. For instance, a spin rod with large-diameter eyes will cast much better than one with small eyes. Large eyes just don't create as much friction on the line during the cast. Conversely, the small eyes of a baitcasting rod

Spin tackle at left has noticeably bigger rod guides, for ease of casting. Baitcaster on right shoots line straighter through the smaller guides.

allow the line (which spools off a considerably smaller reel surface) to straighten out as it pours through the guides.

Most baitcasting rods have a "trigger" so an angler can get a better grip on the rod, using his index finger to wrap around the protruding

part. This helps with alignment when casting, and when using heavy line and a tight drag, where an unexpected strike might rip the rod right out of an angler's hands.

Probably the most important aspect of a fishing rod is its flexibility, or action. This largely determines the potential casting dis-

Matching rod performance against you

A passing school of big bull redfish has everyone in this s[...] "bowed up," regardless of what tackle they're using. How lines were crossed this day has never been fully determin[...]

tance of an outfit and the amount of pressure you'll be able to effectively exert on a fish. A rod with a soft tip is excellent for casting lures to spotted seatrout that have a soft mouth and don't require much of a hookset. Stiffer rodtips provide a better hookset on fish with a hard mouth. They also improve casting in windy conditions, and they're best when using heavier lures. You can find a lot of information about a fishing rod on the little index that rodmakers place just above the reel grip. That's where they list the recommended line strength for the rod, as well as lure weight. These companies have tested their product and determined

cal fish population is a great way to form an opinion on the matter.

The power rating of a rod determines how much lifting it offers. That's important when fighting big fish and trying to move them your way in open water.

these guidelines, so it's a good idea to follow them and avoid using lines that are too heavy.

The power in a rod determines how much lifting it offers. That's important when fighting big fish and trying to move them your way in open water. They can greatly decrease the amount of time you spend on a fish, and that can actually be important when you're releasing them. Rods with real lifting power will often stop big fish in their tracks—while an average rod may hardly keep the fish from taking line. The drawback to more lifting power is a sacrifice in rod flexibility and casting distance. You might add sportsmanship, as well.

Anglers should always determine their requirements, before purchasing a rod. Those that use big, live baits off a bridge for snook

Information on the side of a rod indicates the brand, model, length, action and line class, among other things. Consider these before buying; you want to match the rod with your favorite fishing and tackle requirements.

may prefer a rod with minimal flexibility but maximum lifting power. Fishermen pursuing flounder need a light rod that will feel a gentle bite and is easy to cast throughout the day.

Length also matters. Longer rods in some cases offer greater casting distance, while shorter rods are easier to hold for long periods ---and for battling fish. There are compromises for every aspect of inshore fishing, just as there are extremes. A surf fisherman may prefer a 12-foot rod for throwing heavy lures over breaking waves, or lobbing live sandfleas for pompano some 200 feet out. Back in the bay nearby, someone working 1/4-ounce jigs for the very same pompano will need constant

flicks of the wrist. A little 5- or 6-foot rod would be far more appealing for that job.

As for rod components, most anglers do prefer rods as light as possible, so they're more comfortable to hold. Graphite has replaced solid fiberglass rods, but is more expensive. A *combination* of graphite and fiberglass is light, strong and more affordable.

In most cases, the better the rod's material, the more effective the angler. Graphite is very sensitive, so you'll feel the lure or bait better. You can more quickly react to soft strikes. Fortunately, the price of quality graphite has dropped. You should be able to find a suitable, modern graphite rod for under $100.

Drift fishing with spin gear. Graphite rods are more sensitive to fish strikes, but more expensive. Try using a combination of graphite and fiberglass, which is light and strong.

Matching rod with the job

For most inshore spinning applications, a 6 1/2- to 7 1/2-foot rod is ideal for casting with lures or baits, as shown at left. These rods are long enough to produce a greater sweep with good distance and accuracy, yet short enough to be comfortable during a long day, and while fighting fish with minimal wrist pressure. For surf fishermen, an 8- or 9-foot rod with a medium-heavy action will allow for casting long distances with heavier lures. The big guns, 13- and 14-foot rods, are used for delivering small baits way beyond the surfline, as on the right.

Gorgeous seatrout landed while wadefishing.
This one struck a plastic shrimp and was
soon released.

TACKLE OPTIONS:
Lines

Fishing lines are like lures, in that they attract anglers with catchy names and colors. There are a lot of fishing lines on the market and most are pretty good products, particularly premium brands that cost over $5 and are made for salt water.

The standard nylon monofilament line is still around, and has a huge following. "Mono" stretches, and that allows anglers to make mistakes when fighting fish, when other lines would break. Mono also has a relatively long shelf life, is nearly invisible underwater, is easy to tie knots with, and seats well on a spool. That being said, more modern types of monofilament have been produced. There are now lines composed of standard nylon combined with other materials, like polymers, cofilament and multifilament lines. These lines have monofilament wrapped around a different core material, which makes them stronger, more abrasion-resistant, even thinner in diameter. These specialty lines have specific applications—with advantages and disadvantages.

For instance, a cofilament line with an extremely thin diameter is a great choice for fishing open water when long casts are required. That same thin line will cut easier, so

Braided line at left doesn't stretch and offers a solid hookset. Monofilament line at right stretches and is more forgiving.

it's not a good choice for fishing structure like mangrove trees, dock and pier pilings, or rocks.

There are also major differences between soft and hard mono, with the former having less memory on the spool and being less abrasion resistant. Soft mono is a good choice when fishing open water, while hard mono works better around structure or as leader material near sharp teeth. Hard mono also has a lot of memory, so if left on a spool for long periods it will retain the shape of the spool. That adds up to decreased casting distance and a greater chance the line will tangle.

With mono line, the better the quality, the easier it is to cast and use.

The same is true for braided lines. They're typically made of a woven Spectra (gelspun polyethylene) or other synthetic product to yield a line with an extremely thin diameter, yet with a high tensile strength. That can get you into problems if you spool 30-pound braid onto a reel designed to handle 12-pound mono. That heavier breaking strength encourages anglers to use more drag than the rod can handle, and a broken rod is often the result. Or a messed up drag system in the reel.

Then again, braided line can also be a big advantage, when the same outfit has braid with 10-pound strength—but the diameter of 2-pound test. That thinner diameter allows for longer casts with lighter lures or baits, a real advantage over mono lines of the sametest.

Today's options for fishing lines are many and still growing. New colors arrive on the market and are quick to attract new fans.

A 1/4-ounce lure will sail a lot farther on super-thin line.

Braids are more difficult to tie and require specific knots to prevent coming undone. Unlike mono (where noticing wear on the line is obvious) with braided line the damage is almost invisible. It can be easier here to break off a fish without ever knowing your line was damaged.

In the past, some braided lines used graphite material, and these lines had a tendency to cut into the rod's guides. That product gave braided lines a bad name for a few years, but the new synthetic weaves and ceramic guides on fishing rods have pretty much eliminated that problem.

Fluorocarbon lines have also found a niche in the fishing world, primarily as leader material. In some cases they're used to pack entire reels. Fluorocarbon is varied with each company, but most are nearly invisible in water and weigh more than monos or braids—so they sink quicker. Some fluorocarbons are more abrasion-resistant than others, and some are more pliable and have less memory. Each has advantages and disadvantages that need to be evaluated, but in very clear water, fluorocarbon line as leader material is hard to beat. Since fluorocarbon is heavier than mono, it's great when fly fishing with a sinking fly, when you want the leader to sink quickly. This can be a disadvantage in shallow water over grass, where the line sinks into the grass too quickly, requiring a faster retrieve than normal.

There's a good argument for using different lines. Lines that match local water color may make them less detectable to fish. Given a choice, I prefer a light blue or green line that resembles my home waters.

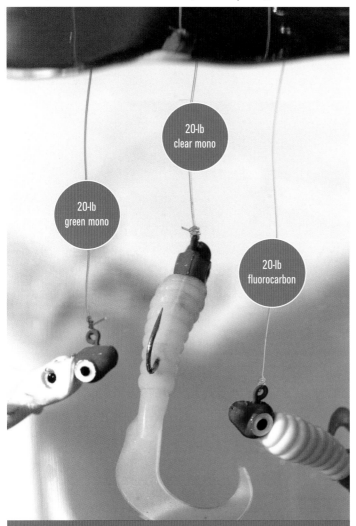

20-lb clear mono

20-lb green mono

20-lb fluorocarbon

Here's something to try: take a 4-inch piece of 20-pound fluorocarbon line and the same diameter of mono. Place them in a clear glass of water. Hold the glass up to the light, and you'll notice the fluorocarbon is harder to see than mono.

Hi-Vis Lines Follow the Leader

Several companies also make extremely bright "hi-vis" lines. Because they're easier to see, they make fighting a large fish easier, because everyone on the boat can follow the line at times. That often means a quicker reaction time against fish that change directions or charge toward structure. The downside to these lines is that fish are likely see the bright colors—so using a clear piece of mono or fluorocarbon as leader is essential.

In many instances a lure or bait moves by a fish at such a rate that they don't have much time to decide whether to eat it or let it go. Debates about line color will continue.

TACKLE OPTIONS:

Hooks

Most hook materials are made to provide strength, durability or to make it easier to sharpen. Stainless steel hooks don't rust, so they last longer (too long) in salt water. They won't rust in a fish's mouth when lost, so bronze or cadmium hooks are perhaps a

Choices on hook design, color and si

F ishing hooks come in a huge assortment of sizes, shapes, components—even several colors.

When measuring hooks or picking them out, remember the scale for measuring fish hooks starts at No. 1 and moves up in numbers to delineate smaller hooks sizes. The larger the number, the smaller the hook. For instance, a No. 8 hook is larger than a No. 10 hook. On the other end of the scale, a 1/0

Live mullet with a circle hook through the nose. This is a very effective arrangement for big redfish.

hook is larger than a No. 1, and the scale for large hooks moves up in size with the number, so that a 10/0 hook is larger than an 8/0 hook.

Hook size is important because too large of a hook will throw off a lure or bait and make it look unnatural. The trick is to find the perfect combination of hook size and weight for a lure or bait—one that's strong enough to hold a gamefish, but doesn't deter a strike. A hook too large may make a lure or bait sink in a suspicious way, alerting a fish that something is amiss.

better choice—especially when fishing around structure.

Properly sharpening hooks is a skill every angler should learn. Many triangulate their hook points with a flat back side, and then a cutting edge on the inside of the gap, much like a knife. This edge provides better penetration than a rounded point—but it can also cut its way out of a fish with soft cheeks, like a striped bass. For bony-mouthed fish like tarpon, a triangulated point is the way to go. For striped bass, snook and seatrout, it's

ontinue to expand. **Experiment and watch what anglers are using.**

better to place the cutting edge on the back side of the hook, not inside the gap, so the hook still has good penetration. Many of the new "chemically sharpened" hooks, with conical points, are not designed for sharpening; they are effective right out of the box.

Colored hooks have made a showing, and they catch their share of anglers. Whether or not they appeal to fish is debatable. Red may make a lure or bait look injured or bleeding, and draw gamefish looking for injured or wounded prey.

The two most important aspects of any fish hook are wire diameter and sharpness. Thin wire hooks penetrate a baitfish with less trauma and are lighter, so the bait can swim around with a hook. With lures, thin wire will also penetrate the mouth of attacking gamefish easier, but it will also bend or straighten under less pressure. For battling fish around structure, thicker hooks work better.

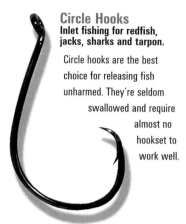

Circle Hooks
Inlet fishing for redfish, jacks, sharks and tarpon.

Circle hooks are the best choice for releasing fish unharmed. They're seldom swallowed and require almost no hookset to work well.

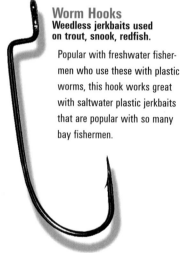

Worm Hooks
Weedless jerkbaits used on trout, snook, redfish.

Popular with freshwater fishermen who use these with plastic worms, this hook works great with saltwater plastic jerkbaits that are popular with so many bay fishermen.

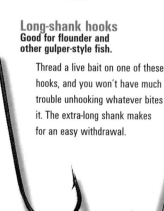

Long-shank hooks
Good for flounder and other gulper-style fish.

Thread a live bait on one of these hooks, and you won't have much trouble unhooking whatever bites it. The extra-long shank makes for an easy withdrawal.

Hook Styles

There are a lot of different hook shapes and opinions vary. For fish hard to hook, have tough mouths or have an ability to spit the hook, I like a Kahle-style hook. It seems to stay in fish well, even with a slack line. Kahle hooks are made of thin wire, so they have outstanding penetration on the hookset. The point is reversed somewhat, turning in toward the eye of the hook.

Another good option is the O'Shaughnessy, a shortshank, livebait hook. This hook is used primarily with live bait, and the relatively short shank allows it to sit against the skin of a baitfish, where it's difficult for gamefish to detect. These hooks are usually made of heavier gauge wire, so they rarely straighten out. They can be used with heavier lines and around structure, where big fish have to be pulled hard.

Circle hooks have their own fans, and own their share of applications. These hooks are a great choice when pursuing fish you plan to release. They're designed to hook a fish in the corner of the mouth of through the lips, and very few are swallowed when used properly. (The offset circle hook doesn't have as good a release record as the straight circle). Remember, you do not set the hook when using a circle hook. Instead, you keep the line tight and lift slowly to apply even pressure. That allows the hook to slide into the corner of the mouth and penetrate, even through a bony tarpon mouth.

When using cut bait, a bait-saver hook, which has small barbs on the back of the shaft, will

help keep the bait on, and prevent it from being nibbled or pulled off by small fish. The bait-saver style is perfect for using with small pieces of shrimp, blood worms, clams, crabs or any small bait items.

There are also good applications for long-shank hooks. When fishing for toothy gamesters like bluefish and Spanish mackerel in clear water (where a steel leader might be ignored by larger, more experienced fish) a longshank hook on a mono leader will keep sharp teeth from cutting through leader.

There are many hook shapes and styles, each with a different application. For a more in-depth look at some of these options, check out *Complete Book of Baits, Rigs and Tackle* by Vic Dunaway.

Small but strong livebait hook used on big fish that love small baits. Throw this in front of a big permit or hundred-pound tarpon and watch what happens.

Livebait Hooks
For trout, snook and other finicky bay fish.

The red color supposedly means blood in the water. The thin diameter doesn't damage a live bait, so it can swim around more naturally.

Kahle-style hooks
Number one chooice for pompano in the surf.

This unusual hook sets itself. Thread a sand flea bait on one of these hooks, and watch a pompano or whiting hook itself simply by bending the rod.

Snell hooks
General purpose hook for many fish species.

This hook can be rigged with a snell knot, which is very strong. That bent hook eye makes for a better hookset.

Heavier livebait hooks
Big redfish, black drum, tarpon, cobia.

Meant for big fish, these hooks simply do not straighten out during a very long battle. Easy to hide in that bait, too.

TACKLE OPTIONS:
Fly Fishing

There are many exciting opportunities for fly fishing inshore waters.

Technology has given us better equipment, but the basics remain the same: anglers still use the weight of the fly line to cast, and try to fool a fish with a small tuft of fur and feathers. They also fight the fish with a very unfavorable line retrieval rate. These elements put the odds in the fish's favor, but the challenge of getting a fish to eat, and then landing it on a one-to-one ratio reel is rewarding indeed.

Casting well in the wind calls for a certain measure of skill with this type of tackle. With fly fishing, it all starts with the perfect cast, which makes the rod the most important item. While the weight of the line

Strip, strip, strip! Angler on point, watching large fish following his fly.

determines how it will react when it leaves the rod, the flex and power of the rod is what makes the delivery.

The classic old bamboo fly rods are just that—classic and old, and they can't compare with modern tackle. They're great for certain fish, however. Or when an angler

The right combination of fly r

Fly fishing tackle has revolutionized
Northeast striper fishing.

e, leader and fly is a true blessing when the fish turn on.

wants to step back in time for a greater challenge, to get a feel for what anglers were once confronted with. For long casts and powerful gamefish, however, a modern graphite or fiberglass rod is superior.

For most inshore applications, a 9-foot fly rod is the best choice for attaining long casts

so typical in open water. Some anglers move up to a 10-foot rod if they do a lot of wade fishing, to compensate for their loss of height above the water. Shorter rods work as well, but limit casting distance. That's why the industry standard is a 9-foot rod.

Fly reels are a different story. I've watched some of these reels explode and fall overboard in pieces from the pressure of a fast-moving fish. I've also seen incredible catches made with reels designed for freshwater panfish. The first tarpon I ever caught on fly was landed with a $28 Pflueger Medalist reel and a graphite fly rod. One fly-casting buddy of mine has less than $100 tied up in his rod, reel and line, and he outfishes me constantly. That being said, a high quality, machined aluminum reel will handle big fish and last many years in a saltwater environment, so they are worth the investment. A quality fly reel should last a lifetime. Many offer small advantages when casting or fighting fish that are valued over the years. For instance, the old-style knuckle-busters that allowed the reel handle to spin with the spool are still the most common fly

This angler keeps a stripping basket on his waist, so the waves won't toss his fly line coils around and mess up his cast.

serious you want to be---or can afford.

Due to the wide size range of fish, and flies used for inshore saltwater fishing, anything from a 6- to a 13-weight rod has its place. Flats anglers seeking to minimize line impact near spooky fish opt for rods and lines in the 6- to 9-weight class, though big tarpon, stripers and sharks call for rods from 10-weight on up. Keep in mind that fly size and fly weight factor in to casting efficiency, so give that primary consideration, along with the size and fighting ability of your target fish when choosing a fly rod.

reel, but an anti-reverse feature makes it easier on your knuckles when fighting fish. Large arbors that allow more line to be retrieved with each turn of the reel handle are a nice advantage as well, but not a necessity.

The last aspect of fly tackle is the backing, which gets to be very important if you hook bigger fish. Fast, hard-running species like bonefish will strip huge segments of line off a reel. It's desirable to have minimal friction in the water over the course of a long fight. Many fly anglers, for their backing, depend on spectra-type braided lines that have a high tensile strength, but also a small diameter. That takes up less

from a reel. Many anglers now prefer large-arbor reels for that job.

space on the reel, which allows for more line capacity, and it's strong enough to put a lot of heat on heavy fish.

As with all tackle, there is no fly-fishing outfit that does everything. As your passion for the sport builds and your skills improve, that's the time to step into the realm of specialty rods, reels and lines that will make chasing one particular fish species an easier task.

The choice of flies and leader materials is another facet of flyfishing that we will cover later in this book. For now, it's important to experiment with several different fly outfits, and develop an educated opinion on the best gear for your area.

Fly Lines

There are major differences among fly lines, and like the differing weights of rods, each line has a specific application for inshore game-fish. Sinking lines get the flies deeper of course, while floating lines keep a fly nicely above a grass bottom. A weight-forward line is probably the easiest to cast and the most commonly used on the coast. Different line colors may make it harder for fish to see the line. Some lines are more compatible with warm or cool temperatures and cast better in those elements. Fly tackle choice is based on experience and what "feels best" for an individual. Give several models a try. Let the gear speak for itself.

CHAPTER 4

Inshore Fishing From Boat or Shore

Every inshore fishing area in this country is unique, because of the variety of fish and different terrain. Some areas will grab your heart, while others turn you off visually—yet they still produce some of the best fishing action for that section of the country.

From marshes to flats, beaches to inlets, fishing is defined by terrain and the fish. All these areas hold some fish, but not all offer great fishing. And perhaps not all of them are for you. Each area does offer variety, challenge and sport to someone, when taken in the right context.

We're very fortunate to have so many fishing options in this country. If you're like most anglers, certain areas have a natural attraction, a spot you love to fish. The more time you dedicate to working that area closely, the greater your fishing knowledge and the better your catch rate.

Let's look at some of those areas and what they really have to offer. A few at least are bound to fit your favorite style of fishing. It's time to broaden your fishing horizons!

Terrain and options for the discerning angler—the whole nine yards.

Wading out from the boat. These anglers are hunting shallow-water bonefish and permit on clear, tropical flats, where fish can be stalked from a distance. They're keeping it sporty by using fly tackle, rather than easier spin gear.

Bays and Estuaries

Some bays may be only a few miles in size, while areas like mighty Chesapeake Bay, that separates Virginia and Maryland, stretch for literally hundreds of square miles. The Indian River Lagoon on Florida's east coast offers 160 miles of outstanding shallow water. Similiar in size is the Laguna Madre in South Texas, which is far more isolated from development.

What makes these bodies such great fishing grounds is their environmental balance. They have giant, natural food chains that begin with the smallest marine life forms and rise up to huge gamefish. Even the biggest fish return to the smallest life forms, as they die off and biodegrade into the food chain. From catfish and stingrays that clean the bottom, to oysters and seagrasses that filter the water, every form of life has a function in this delicate balance of marine life.

The main reason these areas are so rich in sealife is their habitat, and you'll learn that most fish have some ties to habitat, whether to hide from predators or enhance the odds of catching prey. The better the habitat, the healthier the marine life and the more food produced by the system. A strong food chain essentially improves the size and number of gamefish.

Let's look at a system like Chesapeake Bay. Rich in clams, oysters and crabs and dotted with a variety of seagrasses, this bay offers plenty of food and shelter to small fish like kil-

The main reason these areas are so rich in sealife is their habitat.

lifish, croakers and bunker (menhaden). Those species themselves provide food for flounder, red drum, tautog, striped bass, weakfish and bluefish. In fact, many large schools of gamefish encountered in the bay are gathered specifically to take advantage of available food. Remove one element out of the food chain like the blue crab, and gamefish like striped bass and red drum populations begin to suffer. Without food to feed the fish, local stocks decline as the fish migrate into other waters in search of food. Or they die of starvation.

Estuaries are critical nursery grounds for juvenile fish. Many species actually need a low salinity environment in their early stages, with plenty of vegetation and protection from strong tides. Fresh water from rivers contribute to a balance that creates the perfect habitat for shrimp and small minnows, perfect food for small gamefish like red drum and seatrout.

Shallow-water redfish taken on the flats, while drift-fishing. This angler stays dry and uses less energy while in the boat.

The better the habitat, the healthier and more diverse the marine life.

At left, prowling the flats using pushpole power. Anglers below, prefer electric motor in the current.

When shrimp are running out of the marsh and into the open bays of Louisiana, the fish aren't the only critters attracted.

Nowhere is this more true than in the coastal marshes of Louisiana, long famous for growing a large percentage of Gulf Coast seafood.

Only by understanding the natural balance of the bay or estuary you fish, will you get a complete understanding of the habits of its

Even on a chilly day, gamefish are willing to feed on the flats when the sun briefly warms the water.

gamefish. For instance, baitfish runs like the giant walls of "peanut" bunker roaming the shallow flats of Long Island Sound are motivated by water temperature, salinity and tides. When these fish push up into the shallows, the stripers, flounder and bluefish are sure to be behind them. Most baitfish "runs" are cyclic and occur around the same time every year. By keeping track of when these small fish are in the shallows each year, you can easily target gamefish feeding from their ranks. Knowing the size and species of a natural food source, you can use a lure or fly that best mimics that

prey—and that means a greater chance of getting a fish to strike.

The same goes for bait. If small bunker are running and that's what gamefish target on the menu, then throwing a live eel "won't get you spit," as they say in some regions. Tossing out a live, small bunker will obviously hook you up with fish time and again. Understand the food source, and you're halfway there.

This strategy applies no matter what bay or estuary you fish. When shrimp are running out of the marsh and into the open bays of Louisiana, the fish aren't the only critters attracted. Seagulls flock to an area where seatrout are chasing shrimp to the surface. That's when they hover and dive, easily catching shrimp as they skip across the surface. An angler should know that a large flock of birds on the water in November means that seatrout are busting the surface under those birds. Conversely, a flock of gulls during summer means that the menhaden (locally called pogies) are under attack. Or someone dumped a bag of potato chips in the water. Either way, you will notice boats converging at high speed.

Keep in mind, not all food supplies are obvious. Large schools of minnows moving into a bay may not be visible from the surface, but they're sure to attract predators. Flounder and redfish follow minnow schools for miles to take advantage of easy, consistent meals. A flounder in the boat that regurgitates small minnows is a likely sign the entire area is blanketed with these baitfish, and that more flounder may be around.

Probably the greatest factor motivating fish

movements is spawning behavior. When the call of nature beckons, fish gather in great schools to procreate. That doesn't mean the fish stop eating. All that spawning burns a lot of energy, and in many cases the fish are hungrier than ever; they're in large schools that are more competitive and less likely to pass up an offering. These spawning aggregations also offer some of the largest fish of the species, as the big roe-laden females are at their heaviest just before the spawn. Spawning behavior is also cyclic and follows set patterns, and by paying close attention you can take advantage of annual fish runs. Many of the best fishing days occur when these fish are gathered in one area to spawn. Catching and keeping these fish caught in the act of spawning is an ethical dilemma, and many anglers now carefully release their catches.

There are also pre-spawn and post-spawning behaviors to consider. In both cases the fish are ravenous and trying to build or replenish their

Temperature and Salinity

During dramatic changes in water temperature, most gamefish seek out comfort zones, areas that offer an optimum temperature for their metabolic needs. If water temperature drops too fast or far, looking for fish in deep water during prolonged periods of cold weather or at night, and in the shallows during those warming, sunny days, especially late afternoon.

In areas that experience cold winters, like Charleston, South Carolina, redfish become more acclimated to temperature changes. Cold fronts are less likely to make significant drops in water temperature here, as air temperatures don't swing through great changes like they do in South Texas and Florida. In South Carolina, those reds and seatrout adapt to cooler water temperatures, feeding on a more consistent basis.

Redfish head for deeper water when a bad cold front arrives.

some coastal fish become lethargic, and after several days may even die by the thousands. For that reason, many fish move into deeper water each evening when the air and water temperatures drop. Deeper water takes longer to react to temperature changes. Shallow water will cool and warm more quickly.

Most winter days on Tampa Bay, that Florida sunshine beating on the water leads to heat being absorbed into the bottom. It's a warming trend in the shallows, so fish move out of more stable temperatures in the channels and holes, back to the shallows where the sun heats them up. Knowing this, seatrout anglers focus on

Salinity is another big key to finding fish. Species like redfish and seatrout are very adaptable to low salinities, but many of their food sources are not. When mullet are pushed out of the marshes and into Galveston Bay, seatrout follow them into open water. When mullet return to more brackish marshes, the trout and reds are sure to follow.

But not all gamefish are tolerant of changing salinity. Bluefish will move away from fresh water to seek higher salinity, which is always closer to the ocean. Knowing this, an angler targeting blues can eliminate a lot of fishing area that might normally have drawn his attention.

natural body fat, so they can be aggressive.

Once you have a basic knowledge of the habits of food sources and fish species, you can begin targeting specific fish to catch. In any bay or estuary, there are major players and favorites. New England waters have the brutish striped bass and bluefish, both strong, hard-fighting species that are very aggressive in

The water boils with striped bass feeding on the surface. Has anybody got a topwater plug?

shallow water. Almost every bay or estuary has some shallow water to fish; that's where you can wade and throw swimming plugs or bucktails that mimic forage fish. Frigid water doesn't encourage much wading except during summer, so most anglers prefer casting from a boat or shore. Strategies differ on the flats, with most anglers fishing bait on the bottom. Or they cast or slow-troll lures around structure.

Tides play a huge influence in northeastern bays, where immense volumes of water move in and out with every tidal change. Fish move with the water to avoid getting trapped in the shallows, or to find new food. Moving tides create rips and strong currents that wash bait from the shallows. Gamefish know this, so they concentrate in these areas and utilize them as feeding stations. These areas are very common around inlets where bays meet ocean, and are accessible from shore or boat. Since

most gamefish feed facing into the current, it's best to cast lures or baits upcurrent, allowing them to flow naturally with the tide, right into the mouth of a waiting fish.

Each fish species has its own behavioral characteristics. Striped bass prefer to sit in moving water and wait for their prey to arrive with the tide—but they'll also herd baitfish up against a shoreline or island. Bluefish are more random in their foraging, moving almost any direction in the current, but usually traveling in schools composed of like-size specimens (so they don't end up being cannibalized by a larger member of their clan). Bluefish have a habit of eating the tails right off their prey so they can't swim away. Once the tail is gone, bluefish return and eat the rest at their leisure. There's a lot of fallout and waste when bluefish are worked up into a frenzy, with small chunks of baitfish falling to the bottom. Other blues simply scour the bottom for easy morsels, which is why a chunk of bunker or mullet on the bottom is an outstanding bluefish bait.

Flounder may or may not school in one area, but during winter in the upper Atlantic states, these fish can congregate over a specific type of bottom terrain. In many cases, that same bottom typically holds a lot of blood worms, a favored food source for flounder. (On the Gulf Coast, flounder in winter normally migrate each November through the passes, staying a good ways offshore during colder months. A few remain in the bays, where they are subject to sudden shock from severe cold fronts.)

As for weakfish in the Atlantic, those are a schooling fish often looking for one specific water depth and clarity. Once they find that

Tides play a huge influence in northeastern bays, where immense volumes of water move in and out with every tidal change.

perfect habitat, they work as a team to locate the food in the area, and then stick with that food source for weeks at a time. Drop a jig in the middle of a school of feeding "weakies," and you're going to have non-stop action until the tide changes. Or bait shifts into another area. When that happens the fish will move as well, and your honey-hole will suddenly turn sour.

No matter what inshore waters you fish, structure often plays a key role in locating gamefish. Structure may be in the form of bridge pil-ings, docks, oyster bars or grass. It appears in many forms and affects fish in a variety of ways. Structure determines current flow and direc-tion, and creates little feeding areas when water speeds up or funnels bait to hungry gamefish. In the large sounds that blanket coastal North and South Carolina, all these structures are likely to hold fish. Oyster bars provide both food and channel water, offering two very good elements for finding baitfish. Redfish are opportunistic feeders that utilize these oyster structures (that also offer hideouts for tender young crabs). Each bar is a natural barrier to pin baitfish against. Given the choice of jumping onto a dry oyster bar or try-ing to elude attack-ing redfish, a mullet will work to the shallowest point of the bar and then make a break for open water. Redfish station themselves between the bar and open water and have a pretty good chance of catch-ing their meal.

In many coastal areas, seagrass beds provide habitat for shrimp and small baitfish, and fish such as seatrout grow up taking advantage

Anglers at top are working the old dock pilings and finding plenty of action. This healthy bed of bottom grass, often called turtle grass, is home to countless baitfish, crabs and predators.

of these often huge areas. These dense, grassy areas often stretch for miles, laden with millions of small pinfish. But they also provide sanctuary from predators. Young, camouflaged seatrout find safety in the grass from lurking bluefish, so these grassy undersea meadows also double as a safety zone. Over time, trout learn that sandy potholes in the grass make great ambush points for catching prey, as they cross the open sand. As trout become large enough to avoid becoming a meal themselves, these potholes become their favorite ambush points.

The same goes for docks that offer shade and an ambush point for various fish. During the high sun hours, fish can ease under a dock to avoid direct sunlight. While there, they can still expect to find a meal or two. The barnacles and oysters attached to those pilings are hosts to a variety of shrimp, crabs and worms that sheepshead, for instance, love to pluck out. If you drop a small live shrimp along one of those pilings, very likely some sheepshead, trout or redfish is going to think it jumped off the piling, an easy meal.

Most coastal marshes are a combination of mud, sand, shell and grass, exposed to the tides. In these areas, it's the deep holes that hold fish during low tide. The fish push up into the grass and prowl the shorelines during high water. In places like Georgia, a tremendous tidal range moves a lot of water. (Gulf states with isolated bays far from any inlet may have very anemic tides on most days). Grassy areas several feet deep at high tide lose water as the tide recedes, in Atlantic states rather quickly, and even more so in the Gulf—especially if a cold front with strong north winds shoves the water out. This creates small channels of moving water in the grass and pulls food out into open water— drawing feeding fish during outgoing tides. Seatrout, redfish and flounder are commonly found at the mouths of these cuts. In many cases, an angler can spend an entire tide at one location, catching all three species along with a few sheepshead and croakers, until the tide changes.

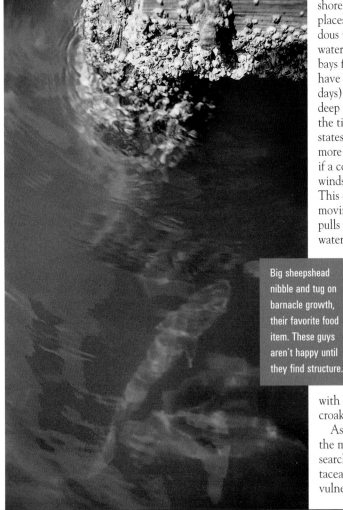

Big sheepshead nibble and tug on barnacle growth, their favorite food item. These guys aren't happy until they find structure.

As water floods back into the marsh, these fish follow, searching out displaced crustaceans, mollusks and baitfish vulnerable in rising water.

Unfortunately, a flood tide also means these fish can disperse over a wide area, so they're much less likely to be concentrated. But a lot of good fish are caught on incoming tides, regardless. In these same marshes, the larger open-water areas with deeper water are where the big shrimp runs take place, as these crus-

Wading angler lands a nice seatrout during "ice cream" weather conditions on a Texas flat.

taceans migrate out during the fall months. This influx of food draws gamefish out of the shallow marsh and into the open bays, where they're more susceptible to fishing pressure. In these circumstances, a live shrimp suspended under a cork is hard to beat for anything, from sheepshead to redfish. You'll also find a lot of bigger fish in open water, particularly redfish that move out of the marsh and into the open Atlantic on a regular basis. These deeper-water

areas offer food and shelter, but also quick access to the ocean, should they feel the need for more space.

Once you reach Florida with those warmer water temperatures, sand bottom and shallow bays and estuaries, like in the huge Indian River Lagoon, anglers really get into wade fishing. That's also true in Texas, where wade fishing is nearly as popular as football.

Because many of these areas are less than three feet in depth, anglers have access to large portions of bay, without need for a boat. Simply pull your car over along a stretch of open water, grab a rod and start walking and wading. Of course, it pays to have some good structure or habitat around to attract the fish.

Here the shallow depths that make wading so easy are also what attract gamefish species like snook, trout, redfish, pompano and flounder. In this case baitfish mostly try to get into the shallowest water possible to avoid predators. Gamefish prowl the edges of these shorelines, often in the shallowest water they can get up into.

In some cases, the best wading spots require an angler to use a boat to cross deep water, to reach a spot not so easily accessible to car traffic. These more remote areas most often offer more fish, and wading remains the stealthiest way to approach them.

These spots also have dropoffs where fish like to hunt. A species like ladyfish, which schools in large numbers, will work one side of a spoil island, and will crush anything that gets in their path. Ladyfish are voracious feeders that love a moving current, so a good, strong tide gets them active.

Wading isn't always an option, especially in areas with soft, mud bottom like Florida Bay on the southern tip of Florida. Here the bottom is so soft, an angler will sink in the mud up to his knees (if not armpits, which is dangerous), eliminating any chance of covering ground. Anglers in much of that bay have to fish from a boat, although a fair number wade hard sand and shell found along mangrove islands and shorelines on its western edges. From a boat, an angler can slowly pole the shallows, hoping to spot a redfish with its face in the grass. A trolling motor helps. Even in deeper water here, that same motor will help ease up to a tripletail floating next to a crab trap buoy.

The diverse mangrove, seagrass and oyster habitat of this bay makes it one of the healthiest ecosystems in North America, and that is reflected in the fish population. During winter months, tarpon over 100 pounds can be seen soaking up the sun in leeward coves. They also move out into open water as they migrate south to the Keys each spring. Those dormant

The diverse mangrove, seagrass and oyster habitat makes Florida Bay one o

tarpon of winter require bait in front of their face, which can be an easy cast. The spring tarpon school and move as one unit, so getting a lure or bait in front of these fish requires more stealth and consistently good casting.

Farther north along the Gulf Coast, bays and marshes of the Florida Big Bend represent a different type of bottom—often made of limestone that will shear the lower unit off an outboard and leave an angler stranded far from shore. These big rock formations are similar to the oyster bars of the Carolinas, though they don't give an inch when hit by a propeller. They do, however, channel water movements with the tides, trapping food and shuttling it from one area to the next.

Redfish in these areas are known for their distinct tidal habits. Fish in one location at low tide will likely pull a repeat on the following day. These fish follow movement patterns for long periods, but that doesn't mean you can easily get to them in shallow, rocky water. If you can access those fish, you'll likely have non-stop action, as they have nowhere else to go, and will sit in those holes until the tide returns.

A similar condition exists on shallow grass-flats, which get extremely shallow with the low spring tides. In these areas, miles of flats will lose all but five or six inches of water for several hours, but large depressions in the flat, some an acre or more in size, will hold three to six feet of water even on especially low days. Most of the fish pouring off these flats move into those holes with the low tide. Find the holes (and return with GPS) and you can catch a trout or redfish on almost every cast until the water comes back in and the fish spread out on the flats again.

In Louisiana's Lake Calcasieu, some of the best fishing structures are spoil islands, those small sand banks dotted with grass that gradually ease into the water. They form sandbars and points which seatrout use as ambush areas for shrimp and baitfish. As with most other estuaries, baitfish (like mullet) try to remain as shallow as possible. Those sand-lined shores offer perfect areas to get into skinny water to avoid predators. But during fall when extreme high tides flood in, big

e healthiest ecosystems in America.

Covering Lots of Ground

When hoping to cover large areas, fishing in a boat is simply the only way to go. In big waters like Long Island Sound, Galveston Bay in Texas or Tampa Bay in Florida, an angler with mobility can relocate with ease. With a boat, you can search multiple spots as you look for the best water conditions. This same strategy works from land, but not nearly as effectively—it's tough to change shorelines without having to drive and deal with traffic and road limitations. By boat, the shortest route between two points on a big bay is often just a straight line, a piece of cake when the weather is nice.

At least two Texas state record trout were caught by wade fishermen who left their boat.

Easing up on the fish at sunrise. There is no better way to sneak up on trophy-size fish in shallow water, than by doing so on foot.

the fights can be a tough battle. At least two Texas state record trout (one stood for many years) were caught here by wade fishermen who anchored and left their boat. Both huge trout no doubt thought they were eating mullet instead of artificial baits. Baffin Bay was fished commercially by trotliners back in the 1960s, who baited up with live pinfish. Eyewitness reports tell of them catching dozens of 12-pound trout in a single night, which isn't a bad average.

During winter, mullet move into the bays and seek those grass flats with adjacent deeper dropoffs, where they can move back and forth from shallow to deeper water with changing weather systems. From February through April, some of the largest seatrout in the world come off these grassflats, and most fall for a topwater or suspending lure that mimics a live mullet. If you're trophy hunting for trout, that's the time to go. Just be sure to release them; fiberglass mounts last for decades.

Most fish species follow set patterns that are driven by food, comfort, reproduction, salinity, tides and other factors. As you dedicate more time to inshore fishing, you will learn these little nuances that allow anglers to better target fish. Many of these patterns become ingrained to the point they become a normal part of the thought process. Other patterns require documentation to keep track of, like a logbook or a fish photograph with the date on it. Sometimes knowing exactly *when* that fish was caught helps an angler return to the same spot each year. One year I bought my first vehicle in early May, and ended up catching some huge snook later that very afternoon. If something like that (new car and snook) jogs your memory, that's a good thing. If not, it's better to keep a fishing log.

trout can move up onto the edges of the island and get into the shallows with the bait. During these periods the topwater action on trout can be some of the best in the world, with multiple limits of trout commonplace.

During summer, deeper areas near those islands provide great ambush zones for trophy trout that are looking for a single large mullet that will satisfy dietary requirements for a few days. While big trout hunt the dropoffs, juvenile redfish roam the shorelines looking for shrimp and crabs on shallower sand bottom.

Deeper parts of Baffin Bay, which is really part of the Laguna Madre in Texas, carry a unique reef system that offers sanctuary and ambush sites for seatrout and redfish. These patches of oolitic limestone also attract mullet and other bait, which trout and reds chase without mercy. Barnacles and other mollusks living on the rocks attract small shrimp and crabs, which in turn attract sheepshead and black drum. Though moving water here is often nil, structure and food mean that most inshore species are attracted. Here the big key is to match baitfish species with a lure of similar size and shape. The strikes are vicious and

Capt. Gregg G

A heroic battle with a
44-inch snook landed on
8-pound test line in
Stuart, Florida. Fish was
released seconds later.

Inlets and Passes

If bays and estuaries hold the greatest populations of fish, it's only common sense that inlets and passes leading to the sea would be a natural funnel for most inshore species. These funnel higher salinities, moderating temperatures and often better water quality. Some of the largest fish in the country find those conditions very agreeable.

These are also food superhighways, as strong currents sweep every form of forage back and forth. When food is plentiful such as during a shrimp run, you can bet gamefish will be there. Inlets lead to large bodies of open water and certainly offer a wider variety of species, some of which don't care much for shallow bays. Big sharks, king and Spanish mackerel, large red and black drum, cobia, bonito and other predators that normally prefer deep water, make regular visits to inlets to feed on bait runs. Big spawner-size striped bass and red drum leave inshore estuaries once they reach maturity.

They rarely visit back inside, but they can be commonly found in deeper (often rock jettied) inlets around the country. Huge hammerhead and bull sharks visit those inlets and passes on the west coast of Florida, to feed on tarpon migrating into these waters every spring. A 15-foot hammerhead inside the bay on shallow flats would be a very rare sight, though it happens in the Keys every year. As for those deeper inlets, anything could be down there.

On outgoing tides, water pours out from estuaries and bays, with a lower salinity than ocean water. These tidal differences can have big impacts on gamefish. Species that prefer clean, warmer, higher salinity water from the ocean will visit these inlets on an incoming tide. The moment that tide changes, cooler water with perhaps lower salinity may move those fish back offshore.

During spring and fall, tides are stronger than normal and huge volumes of water move through, often doubling the current's velocity. If these tides coincide with schooling baitfish or migrating shrimp or crabs, the inlet will turn into one joyous food chain, with fish eating shrimp, and larger fish eating smaller fish, and sharks whacking the largest gamefish. (It's great to be at the top of the food chain).

A good example of a famous inlet is Montauk

Inlets are also food super-highways, as strong currents sweep every form of forage back and forth. When food is plentiful, you can bet game-fish will be there.

See DVD for more on inlets and passes.

Rocky jetty provides action for light-tackle angler. The rocks below are tough on that tackle, however.

Point, the northern end of Long Island, New York, and the largest opening into Long Island Sound. A lot of fish species, including striped bass, bluefish and flounder, spend their early stages in the shallows here, learning to forage while remaining safe from predators. As these species reach maturity, they join schools of their clan, which regularly migrate out of the Sound and into the open Atlantic.

When the tide is really moving and sweeping food along, sportfish feed facing into the current, often holding their position. In many cases they seek out rocks or breaks in the current they can sit behind, watching for food, lunging into the current for a bite. Knowing this, anglers should fish with the current, just like moving baitfish. Whether using big plugs, jigs or live bait, the key to fishing an inlet or pass is getting your offering to sweep along in the current to waiting fish. For that reason, most anglers make their casts up-current and then work the offering back toward them,

moving along with the water flow. As the lure or bait gets downcurrent and stops, it should be reeled in and cast back upcurrent.

In areas where there are large eddies created by underwater structure, sandbars or shallows, bait will sometimes get pushed into these features by the current, where gamefish feed on their ranks. In this scenario the best method is again to follow the same path as the food source, casting up-current and then letting it sweep along until it enters the eddy, and then working it back in to shore. Quite often the strikes come in very shallow water or just as the bait is at your feet.

Another option for inlet fishing is to anchor and set out a spread of four live or dead baits, using heavier tackle, such as 4/0 gear, with 100-

Tide ripping out means the fish are likely turned on. Waders beware of dropoffs and currents during these conditions.

Strong, incoming tide at sunrise. Try drift-fishing or anchoring within casting distance of structure.

pound leaders and circle hooks. Lead weights are changed to match the current's velocity, to effectively anchor those baits in a U-shaped spread behind the boat. Action often takes place in a fairly strong current, and it requires muscle to crank in those "bull" redfish, tarpon, sharks, big stingrays and large jack crevalle. (Tough work, but somebody has to do it.)

Currents moving from sound to ocean can be swift, and most bait species can't navigate them except near the shoreline, where rocks often slow the current's flow. Those same rocks that block the current also give cover to trout,

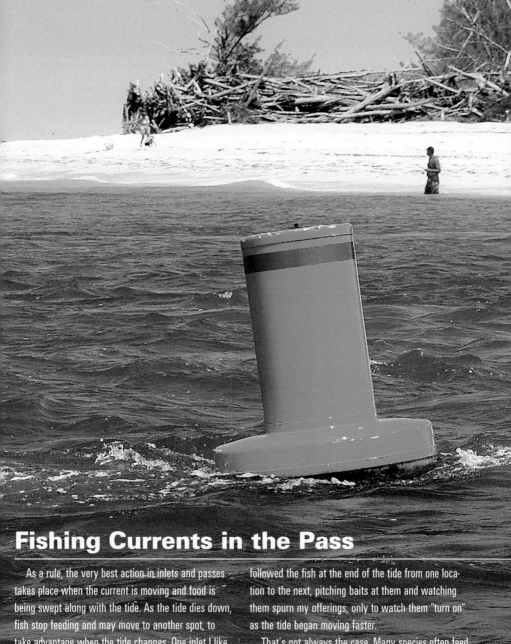

Fishing Currents in the Pass

As a rule, the very best action in inlets and passes takes place when the current is moving and food is being swept along with the tide. As the tide dies down, fish stop feeding and may move to another spot, to take advantage when the tide changes. One inlet I like to fish in Southeast Florida holds several large schools of snook during the summer spawning season. These fish follow distinct habits that are tide-motivated, with a school sitting on one section of the inlet on the incoming tide, and then moving about 100 yards to another spot when the tide turns around. I've regularly followed the fish at the end of the tide from one location to the next, pitching baits at them and watching them spurn my offerings, only to watch them "turn on" as the tide began moving faster.

That's not always the case. Many species often feed on a slack tide, with sheepshead, snapper, flounder and sharks just a few that will still readily grab baits during slack water. This is also a time when it's easiest to keep a bait in one location, so that a rock or hole known to hold fish can be worked over during the entire slack period.

Natural inlet without rock jetties, still a good spot when the tide is running out and the water is clear.

Because inlets and passes are subject to erosion, many are lined with rock jetties or seawalls.

Fish hanging around the jetty rocks face into the current, waiting for food to sweep past.

stripers, bluefish and flounder, that move in for the kill. At times the water can be boiling with feeding fish, and a nice striper on one cast may be followed by a monster bluefish on the next.

When these feeding frenzies happen, you never know what you're going to catch, but you can directly target some species. If you want flounder, keep that bait right on bottom.

If bluefish are raiding baitfish on top, then tossing a surface lure, flashy spoon or light-weight jig will increase the odds of "raring back" into a big one.

Because inlets and passes are subject to water erosion, many (if not most) are lined with rock jetties or seawalls. That helps keep the current going, flushing the bay, and prevents the inlet from sanding shut. These same rocks and seawalls are coated with marine growth that attracts small fish, shrimp, crabs and barnacles—all natural bait for gamefish. They also provide a solid (though often slippery) position for walking anglers, who often rack up stringers of big fish from water up to 40 feet deep. As a warning, rock jetty access ranges from the impassible (jumbled boulders) to the pedestrian-friendly sidewalk and safety rail. Jetties somewhere between those extremes grow algae, barnacles, even cruel oysters, all waiting to trip an angler during a moment of carelessness. Veteran jetty anglers can often be picked out by the proud scars they still carry.

Many inlets have a combination of rock and seawall, like Palm Beach Inlet in Florida. Fish use the rocks to hide, while anglers use the seawall for firm footing. Mangrove snapper and snook hold tight to these rocks, where they search for food. As baitfish tire in the main current and move up against the rocks, they become easy prey in their weakened condition. In this case, it's best to cast parallel to shore, and work your lure or bait along the edges of the rocks where a big snook can ambush bait. This can be more difficult when fishing from a boat, as it can be a dicey proposition, anchoring when there is near-constant current and wave action. If the boat ends up in those unforgiving, granite rocks it will ruin your day. Anchoring safely within good casting distance of the rocks takes experience. Many anchors are lost down in the rocks, as well.

Some inlets have bridges spanning them, such as Sebastian Inlet on Florida's Atlantic coast. This inlet also has a rock jetty on the north side, with a man-made steel and concrete fishing pier placed on top of the rocks and out into open water. Just about every fish that swims in the nearby Indian River will move through this inlet at one time or another. Big snook and redfish holding around those bridge fenders and off the end of the jetty are legendary.

A lot of inlets are in remote areas only accessible by boat or with a four-wheel-drive vehicle. Hatteras Inlet in North Carolina or the west end of Dauphin Island, Alabama are good examples. These areas are remote enough to make them inconvenient to get to, but they see less fishing pressure. They're worth the visit, however.

In the fall when those strong, incoming tides and first winter storms bring rough water to the inlets, fishing can be outstanding. Big red drum arrive from offshore, targeted by anglers using large swimming plugs or natural baits. Some of the largest fish of the year are caught then, by anglers soaking baits on the edge of a current. Or casting along a nice steady-flowing shoreline.

At the same time of year, weakfish arrive in the inlets of New England, where a white bucktail jig can produce trophy fish on every cast until the fish stop feeding or move away with the tide. The key to inlet fishing is to put in your time and to follow established feed-ing patterns. Gamefish are creatures of habit, and they may be off by a week or two on their annual run. When they do arrive in the inlets, patient anglers are there—for the first part of the run that usually gets the best action.

Part of the fun of fishing these areas is just getting there. Driving down a remote stretch of beach in a four-wheel-drive vehicle, watching for breaking fish or a good-looking offshore trough between sandbars is about as good as it gets. On those cold fall or spring mornings when the air is crisp and the ocean angry it just feels like something big should be feeding along the beach. When you arrive at one of these areas (at the end of the road) like Montauk Point in Long Island, the reward can be the fish of a lifetime. It's just you and a handful of others willing to put forth the effort to find those fish and be there for the bite. It's trips like these that create lasting memories for all participating anglers.

Amazing fish are caught by anglers walking the jetty rocks, who pay their dues with occasional scratches and scrapes from a slip or fall.

Surf Fishing

Surf fishing is what you make of it. Many surf anglers see the beach as a place to relax, hang out and catch a few rays (sun) and maybe a few fish. Others see the surf as a source of hardcore fishing adventure. Both groups have their arguments, but in the end it's up to the individual angler how intense they make that surf fishing experience.

I'm a big fan of pompano fishing, and know I only need two or three fish to feed my family. When I want to chase these fish, I simply grab two of my 14-foot surf rods, sand spikes, a bag of frozen sandfleas for bait and a lawn chair, and head for the beach. It's great to set out both rods, take a seat and sip morning coffee. Every now and then I get up and check the baits or reel in a fish. By the time bathers and kids begin to arrive, I've got a few fish for dinner and my suntan is improved.

In my case, the key to success is having the right equipment. The 14-foot rods allow me to cast those little sandfleas far enough to reach the back of the outside sandbar, which is where pompano often congregate and feed. At certain times pompano travel closer to the

beach, swimming right along the shoreline trough (in the first "gut") where they can be targeted with a small rod and the same baits. Those days usually take place during spring when the fish are moving north, and an angler with a 6-foot rod can compete against the long rods. Eight times out of 10, however, the long rods prevail against pompano.

There are other days when surf fishing means driving long stretches of open beach looking for fish or hiking in with all your gear, to reach spots that don't offer easy access but hold lots of fish. These trips are just as fun and rewarding; the fish you catch are the products of more strenuous efforts. Camaraderie is just as intense, walking back to the car with your gear and a 40-pound striper in tow.

Surf fishing is also popular because it's productive. Whether you're after jumbo blues or spotted seatrout, the fishing is just as challenging. Many surf fishermen wade out to improve their casting reach, too. In Texas, they often wade out to shoulder-deep water, using a 30-foot stringer for their caught fish, in case a shark appears. Mullet-imitation plugs and flashy spoons are stored on their hat, which is often a Styrofoam pith helmet that floats—and protects from the sun.

Probably the most common method of surf fishing is with bait, where an angler casts out a live eel, clam, chunk of cut bait or even a live baitfish, places the rod in a sand spike and

Fish feeding in the surf likely haven't seen a lure in some time, and will rea

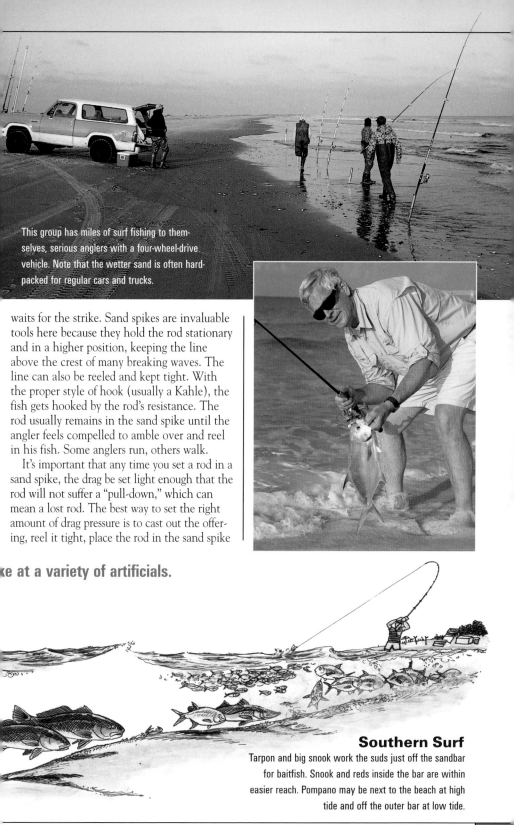

This group has miles of surf fishing to themselves, serious anglers with a four-wheel-drive vehicle. Note that the wetter sand is often hard-packed for regular cars and trucks.

waits for the strike. Sand spikes are invaluable tools here because they hold the rod stationary and in a higher position, keeping the line above the crest of many breaking waves. The line can also be reeled and kept tight. With the proper style of hook (usually a Kahle), the fish gets hooked by the rod's resistance. The rod usually remains in the sand spike until the angler feels compelled to amble over and reel in his fish. Some anglers run, others walk.

It's important that any time you set a rod in a sand spike, the drag be set light enough that the rod will not suffer a "pull-down," which can mean a lost rod. The best way to set the right amount of drag pressure is to cast out the offering, reel it tight, place the rod in the sand spike

…e at a variety of artificials.

Southern Surf

Tarpon and big snook work the suds just off the sandbar for baitfish. Snook and reds inside the bar are within easier reach. Pompano may be next to the beach at high tide and off the outer bar at low tide.

Atlantic anglers with sand spikes and long surf rods wait for action on a breezy day.

and then pull out the drag by hand. The drag should be light enough that a fish can easily take line, but tight enough that the wave action won't pull drag and make the line go slack.

Keep in mind, not all fish in the surf are big. Some of the tastiest catches are whiting and croakers, fish that average only a pound or so, but great table fare. These fish roam the

troughs, have voracious appetites and travel in schools, so where you find one there will likely be more. They're not much of a fight on a long surf rod. On light tackle they can be scrappy, and a blast to throw jigs at while walking along the beach.

Which brings up another form of surf fishing, casting lures to schooling fish. This is the

Northern Surf

Big "chopper" bluefish and always-beloved striped bass are the two key players in northern waters.

sport that attracts big crowds of fishermen to the mid-Atlantic and New England coasts. It's practiced to a lesser extent in the South, where 100-pound tarpon are possible from shore—dwarfing any fish found farther north except for sharks. In the mid- and upper-Atlantic, bluefish, striped bass and red drum prowl the beaches in big schools, dogging baitfish, most often menhaden. The size of these northern predators makes it all but impossible to use the 14-foot rods utilized for pompano fishing; a big fish can put a lot of pressure on an angler's arms, maybe wearing them out completely. Instead, an 8- or 9-foot rod with a medium-heavy action is preferable. This size range can withstand the force of casting a heavy lure, can produce sufficient distance to get to the fish, yet is short enough to make it a lot easier for an angler to reel in a 30- to 50-pound fish or two.

A shock leader is still needed, but the main line strength may be heavier, since it will not be as exposed to currents for prolonged periods.

With this type of fishing, anglers try to use lures that imitate local baitfish. If the fish are

Surf snook landed and ready to take home during the open season in Florida.

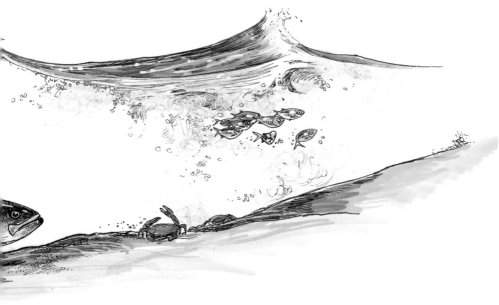

chasing one-pound mullet, then a 10- to 12-inch swimming plug with a side-to-side swagger is the offering of choice. If the fish are after menhaden (locally called bunker), a big spoon might be a better option.

Not all surf fishing requires long rods or heavy tackle. In the Gulf of Mexico, especially Florida and Texas, anglers regularly wade out into the surf—which normally doesn't feature swells like those found rolling off the Atlantic. These guys cast lures or flies with the same light tackle normally reserved for the bays. Calm surf conditions allow for the lighter gear, and the action can be outstanding.

In Florida, snook roam the beaches from late spring through early fall, and anglers can walk the beach and sight-cast to moving schools. Other times the fish hold on structures like small rockpiles or downed trees, and will ambush any lure or bait swimming past the structure. In this scenario, the fish usually hunt deeper troughs, using the shoreline to pin baits up against the sand. The most effective fishing strategy is to step into the water several yards and then cast parallel to shore, so the lure or bait swims along the edge of the trough. Snook charge the baits as they get close to the sand.

In Texas and Louisiana, spotted seatrout and redfish prowl open Gulf beaches, followed by "pluggers," anglers tossing artificial plugs. Other species like Spanish mackerel, blacktip sharks, jacks and ladyfish may mix in, so that angler are often rewarded with a variety of action. As with other areas, it's baitfish that concentrates predators along the beach. Anglers there look for flipping mullet, mostly. In reasonable weather, some of the best action in the country can be had on these remote barrier islands and seashores, far from the crowds.

Isolated, rocky structure attracts fish on all sides.

Reaching Out to

The common denominator in surf fishing is casting distance. More often than not, the longer the cast, the better the chance of covering water or reaching fish. You're going to need a shock leader to keep the line from breaking from the force of the cast, or from cutting into your fingers from the bottom rig's weight. For most surf fishing, anglers use a lighter line on the reel spool and then a heavier shock tippet. The lighter line has a thinner diameter than the leader, and thus can be cast farther. It also has less friction or drag in a current. That can make the difference between your sinker holding bottom for prolonged periods, or washing down the beach and back to shore.

For pompano fishing I prefer a 15-pound line, which allows for casting well over 100 yards with a 4- or 5-ounce sinker. If I use just 15-pound line without a leader, the force of the cast will often break the line if I'm only a fraction of a second late letting go. To combat this, a 30-pound shock leader is tied to the line between the pompano rig and the main line. This wind-on leader is long enough to make six to 10 wraps around the reel spool, through the rod's length and about three feet beyond the rod tip. That's enough for a good arc to the cast. During the pressure of the cast, when the rod is bent from the weight of the sinker, the 30-pound shock leader absorbs the energy much better than 15-pound test. That heavier line pulls the lighter line off the reel for a nice, long cast.

The shock leader has a second purpose—helping drag fish up on the beach. When a fish is hooked, it's fought on 15-pound main line until it nears shore. The heavier line then allows an angler to control the fish better, and to lock down onto the reel spool with his thumb and slowly walk backwards in order to pull the fish from the water with a well-timed wave.

Big Ones in the Surf.

Wade Fishing

Crouching low after wading within casting distance of foraging gamefish. No need to scare fish with a high profile.

Like surf fishing, wading involves getting in the water at some point. Just the water's touch reveals what the water temperature is like—if it's cold the fish may be lethargic and the lure's retrieve needs to be slowed. If it's warm enough, then a topwater plug is suddenly a viable option.

Wade fishing is inexpensive when compared to other styles of inshore fishing, available just about anywhere there's firm enough bottom to stand on. But that's not why it's so popular. Most anglers wade because it's probably the most productive means of catching fish in inshore waters.

Look at Texas—they have some of the most progressive anglers in the country. They have many hardcore fishermen who grow up learning their local waters and the habits of trout, redfish and flounder. Many of these guys have specialty boats designed to cross those big bays, which get very choppy. Yet, their boats have a shallow enough draft to cruise long distances in a foot of water, where the angler can anchor and wade.

For these guys, the boat is just a means of getting there. Once at the spot, most of them jump overboard. They spread out and wade in a line, plugging steadily and stringing fish.

Most hard bottoms with good fish habitat (and baitfish) are targets for anglers who wade. The low profile and silent approach of a wader offers few chances for mistakes, compared with boaters. Unfortunately, many good fishing areas have a soft bottom, and that limits wading. (Soft bottom, besides hindering mobility, may

See DVD for more on wade fishing.

equate with cruel oysters, stingrays and a sore lower back).

In the Florida Keys, the firm sand with grass and clear water makes for the ideal wading venue. There are countless productive flats here to stalk bonefish and permit, though they may not be the most productive. In reality, most of the best flats are covered with silt and "itch mud" several feet deep, that will sink a wade fisherman perhaps to his waist with every step. And then the itch sets in: Little parasites in the silt and grass bite or sting the angler's legs, so that he spends more time scratching than fishing.

For traveling anglers, however, wade fishing is the best option for inshore fishing—one that can really produce some remarkable catches. I've traveled all over Florida and caught fish while wading around many of the towns. Very often I hadn't planned on fishing, but had a rod in the car, a little free time and pair of tennis shoes I wasn't particularly fond of. By the time the trip was over, I'd fished new areas, had some great success and owned the worst pair of sneakers on any three coasts.

One of the first things I learned about fishing is that long casts increase the chances of catching fish, and that same tenet applies to wade fishing. Even though an angler presents a lower profile, the long cast covers more ground and reaches more fish. It also

allows anglers to target more potholes (if he can see them) holding fish.

Pothole fishing is a real kick. That's when anglers wading over thick grass look for sand or mud holes in the grass and specifically work those areas. Inshore predators like seatrout and snook certainly prefer to sit in these holes, as opposed to dense grass, and use these areas to ambush prey. As fish, shrimp and crabs move out of the grass and cross a pothole, they become obvious targets. Their movements can be tracked, their distance measured from safety. Knowing this, predator fish "camp out" in these potholes and wait for marine food to cross that open water. Then they lunge after it.

Pothole fishermen stalk the flats, casting to every sand or mud hole they see, often in less than two feet of water. Because the water is so shallow, fish are more susceptible to predation from sharks and

Staking the boat out and wading the flats. Is there a better way to stalk fish?

Live-baiter with towed minnow bucket wades away from his boat, catching fish.

birds, so they're spookier and harder to approach. But a long cast to a pothole can often draw a strike from a fish that had no idea the angler was even in the area.

Another wading strategy involves blind casting. That may mean casting along a dropoff, over a dense grass bed or spoil bank, sandbar or reef. With blind casting, anglers spend more time searching for fish. This means fan-casting, or completely blanketing an area with casts

until fish are found. The theory here is that by covering every foot of water, you'll eventually find something interested in eating. But that's not always the case.

When I do the blind casting game, I use two rods, one with perhaps a soft-bodied jig, and another with a hook and live shrimp. I stick the rod I'm not using in the back of my waders, and can switch out rods at will. I use the jig to find the fish by blind casting over a large area.

Peaceful, Easy Wade Fishing

A lot of the best inshore fishing takes place in thin water, in areas that are almost unapproachable by boat, so wade fishing is the only option. Redfish, seatrout, flounder and snook push up into the shallows during the warm months to feed, often with their backs out of the water. Sometimes fish are in a deep trough on the back side of a shallow sand or oyster bar, a

spot that won't allow a boat to get in. That means hoofing it. Some of these areas involve grassy or rocky areas difficult to fish without using a weedless lure, like a jerkbait or spoon. The fish nose up into the shallows, looking for shrimp and crabs exposed to the incoming tide, and by the time water floods an area enough to float a boat, the fish have pushed up even farther onto the flat beyond casting range.

Scanning thin water for signs of fish. It's like assuming the hunting traits of a blue heron.

The jig covers a lot of ground in a short time. Using natural bait would require about three times the effort. Once I hook a fish on the jig, I'll put that rod down and switch out to a live shrimp, casting to the same area where the fish was hooked. If a school of trout or redfish are in that area, they're more likely to chase the natural bait than the lure. If I don't catch a fish after several casts, then I'll go back to the lure.

Gamefish become quite wary in thin water, so accurate casts (that don't land on the fish's head, causing a spook) will draw more strikes. If the fish has its face buried in the grass like redfish often do, then the lure or bait has to land close enough to see, but far enough away that the sound of the lure hitting water won't spook. Sight casting can be highly rewarding, perhaps more so than any other means. It's a combination of hunting and fishing.

In cold water climates, shoreline food obviously is different. It might be clams, bloodworms or a host of baitfish species or other food items. It may be over sand bottom without much structure. Open water blind casting is a tough road to hoe, so to speak, and requires patience. It's better to focus on areas where fish are feeding at the surface—or at least showing themselves. Still, if you know there is a good supply of food, you can be sure that stripers, bluefish and weakfish won't be far off.

During winter months, inshore fish generally

Striped bass favor chilly water, and this angler is well protected with warm clothing and chest waders.

migrate toward deeper water—since deeper holes, channels and rivers have more consistent water temperatures than the flats. During warm periods between cold fronts, they often ease back into shallow water, however. Fish spend a lot of time in these deeper areas in winter, and really concentrate there during

> **Most gamefish can't even get into the shallow water that baitfish are capable of, with the exception of bonefish, flounder or small redfish.**

cold fronts and weeks of frigid weather. Knowing this, anglers can wait for the fronts to move through, and then work the deep holes by wading up to them.

There are lots of shoreline structures to consider. Mangrove trees with their intricate root systems offer shelter and shade, very common in South Florida. Rock formations are found in almost all coastal states, including seawalls. But in most cases, the appeal of almost any shoreline is the shallow water that allows bait freedom of movement with a limited threat of

being eaten. Most gamefish can't even get into the shallow water that baitfish are capable of, with the exception of species like bonefish, flounder or small redfish. Bait finds safety in the shallows, but it doesn't last. Because of tidal influence, baitfish, shrimp and crabs have to be mobile enough to seek deeper water when the shallows go dry. Gamefish know this, so they hunt the edges waiting for food to move. They're looking for easy prey.

Along shoreline structure like mangrove trees, which offer a tangle of roots for small fish

Happy angler lands a shallow water redfish. This may not be the peak moment for an angler's day, but it's close enough.

and crustaceans to hide among, gamefish cruise the root's edges, hoping to spook their food into the open. A lure or bait cast parallel to this structure will often draw the attention of any fish on the prowl.

Casting parallel to shore when wading is a common strategy for fishing almost any shore-

Hours of casting artificial plugs reveals which ones really are "killer baits."

line. In some cases, it might pay to cast back out into open water or to fan-cast the entire area. More often than not, however, the best fish are swimming along the shore—in water just deep enough to cover their backs. That's where they ambush small prey that are moving out to deeper water with an outgoing tide.

No matter what form of wade fishing you prefer, you will find that being in the water with the fish brings you a lot closer to nature, and forms a natural bond with your environment. It's a learning experience that is certain to improve your fishing.

If you're going to spend much time wade fishing, you're going to wind up using either lures or live bait. That doesn't mean you won't use both, but one of the two will have more appeal on a regular basis. Neither is the wrong choice and each is different.

Lures allow an angler to cover a vastly bigger area in a day's time, than while using live bait. They're also more convenient to use. It's a lot easier to place a few lures in your pocket and wade out from shore, than to purchase or catch bait, load up a bait bucket and then drag it out to the spot.

Lures are designed to cover all levels of the water column, and artificials chosen should imitate natural baits in your area. If some veteran wader carries his plugs and spoons on his hat or where they can be seen, take note. Very likely they're all "killer baits," or were at one time.

Topwater plugs work great in shallow water or for species that spend a lot of time feeding on top, but that same lure might not work for flounder, which live literally on the bottom. For flounder, a jig or deep-diving plug might be a better option. We'll cover more about lure choices and their applications later in the book. For now, think about whether you want to cover more ground or spend time working over every inch of a given area.

If you decide you want to spend more time live baiting with shrimp, pilchards or any other baitfish, you're going to have to get some special gear to hold the baits and keep them fresh and lively at all times. In this case, a fisherman is only as good as his bait, so you want to present the healthiest, liveliest and best looking bait possible. The nice thing about live bait is that once fish grab it and realize it's the real thing, they don't want to let it go. With lures, a fish might take a swipe at the lure and feel the unnatural bait and not return. Or it may sense that something is not quite right with the lure, and follow it for long periods but never eat. With live bait, it's the real deal, and most fish decide they want it after looking it over.

Jetties and Rocks

Just about anywhere there's an inlet or the potential for high surf to move large volumes of sand, you're likely to find a rock jetty or groin. These man-made structures are designed to impede the water flow and keep sand from shifting down the beach, creating shoals that block boat traffic or produce swimming hazards. While they're built to serve a single purpose, they have a second function and that's to provide structure and habitat for marine life. As you know, most forms of structure will attract fish and other marine life looking for sanctuary, which in turn attracts bigger fish looking for a meal. It's the same with these rocky structures, which often bring the fish right up near dry land. A striped bass or red drum chasing bait up against the rocks knows that bait has only one avenue of escape, and that's directly back at feeding fish. Or they can jump up on dry land, which they sometimes do.

Because these structures are open to the elements, they can be very slippery, with marine growth that can cut through clothing or waders, so it's extremely important to watch where you step on these rockpiles. Those same rocks that can cut through your jeans can easily sever fishing line. That means an angler has to play a fish carefully to keep it out of the rocks, and find a spot to land it without wave action spoiling everything, including injuries.

You'll also find that many of these areas require long walks from the car. Jetties that project several hundred yards out into the ocean can make for a long hike with all your gear, so you have to learn to be more com-

Big critters hang around the jetty rocks, such as this trophy snook.

While they're built to serve a single purpose, jetties have a second functio

See DVD for more on jetties.

This jetty outcropping isn't exactly foot-traffic-friendly, but judging by the crowd of eager anglers, something is going on here. Notice the heavier tackle.

pact, more mobile. Many anglers use metal carts to carry their gear, if a sidewalk is available. Others simply leave a lot of stuff in the car, and carry only what they think they need. If they find they left something in the car, they can always walk back and retrieve it.

The thing to remember about jetty fishing is that the structure attracts fish—and in many cases the best fishing is right at your feet, not over the open sand bottom away from the structure. When waves are crashing against the rocks and roiling the water, baitfish get confused, and that's when larger predators pick them off.

However, fishing around the rocks isn't easy. Expect to lose tackle, for instance, but that's just part of the game. The rocks attract fish, but they also end up keeping

d that is to provide structure and habitat for marine life.

A number of species are especially fond of hanging around jetty rocks. Since sheepshead depend on barnacle growth for their diet, they're always around. Count in redfish, trout (in the Gulf of Mexico), snook and flounder. Look here for stripers and bluefish in the Northeast.

The only true jetty in Louisiana is at Sabine Pass on the Texas border. A boat is required to reach it, and many a fine trout has been dragged up on this low concrete apron. It's now more visible to boaters at high tide, with a few concrete boulder piles.

Fish that work the outer fringes of inlets are now within casting range. Only a surf pier offers the same shots at bigger fish from offshore.

"We don't need no stinkin' boat..." these anglers have parked their car and hit the sidewalked, traffic-friendly jetty in Jupiter, Florida. Below, a stringer of trout and pompano at the Port Aransas jetty in South Texas.

your rigs. It's a trade-off you have to make.

A lot of fishing strategies used around the jetties are similar to those in most inlets and passes, which is to cast your lure or bait upcurrent and work it back with the tide. Fish the eddies, and cast parallel to the structure whenever possible. But those are only a few of the more common strategies here.

Some jetties stick far offshore, providing anglers access to water far from the beach. Beachfront groins offer the same type of opportunities, though they're shorter. In many cases, these structures still provide access to fish like king or Spanish mackerel, cobia, permit, snapper and grouper. Fish that may work the outer fringes of inlets are now within casting range.

For most jetty and rockpile applications, standard light tackle just won't cut the mustard, so to speak. Many fish around the jetties are too strong and can reach the rocks—or strip a reel clean. Most jetty and rockpile fishing is done with medium-heavy rods and reels capable of holding 300 yards of 20- to 30-pound line. The average rod is eight to nine feet long, to provide extra casting distance.

A good landing net with a long handle is another popular item on a jetty. (You'll make a lot of jetty friends, if you have a good net and know how to use it). After all, if someone

Since the tidal exchange at inlets shuttles a lot of food, jetties are essentially structures fish can utilize as sanctuary or feeding grounds. Match this huge draw of fish with minimal fishing pressure, and the action

Since the tidal exchange at inlets shuttles a lot of food, jetties are essentially structures fish can utilize as sanctuary or feeding grounds.

does get a fish close to the rocks, they'll need a way to land it. Rocks closest to the water are wet most of the time and very slippery. Depending on the jetty's design, you often can't get any closer than four or five feet from your fish. A long-handled net makes it easy and helps prevent untimely slips and potential injuries.

Not all the best jetty fishing is done while walking the structure itself. Very often the best jetty fishing is done from a boat. (Places like the Fernandina jetty on the Florida-Georgia border are a jumble of boulders, impossible to walk on. Those daily 6-foot tides bury much of the jetty every day). Boaters can always drift or anchor within casting distance, however. Anglers spend a lot of time doing so, with great success. Since a lot of inlets in this country don't have easy access from land, they get minimal fishing pressure. If they happen to be accessible only by boat and are remote enough, they can be the most productive fishing grounds you will ever find.

can be fantastic on any given day.

Texas, for instance, has a lot of these jetties, with every inlet in the state lined with flattop granite rocks (except one, Pass Cavallo, left to

On the Rocks

Some of the best fishing around the rocks occurs during the worst weather, which admittedly can be hazardous to boats. High winds and seas really move a lot of water around these structures, and push a lot of the food into the open. Fish sense this, and move close to wave-crashing rocks to feed. Some of the best fishing in Florida takes place right after a hurricane, as the fish move in close to the beach to feed on all the bait pushed out of the inlets.

Fishing the jetties with a boat can be a dicey proposition in choppy conditions, and it requires an alert crew if the boat should drift too close to the rocks.

nature). Some jetties there have very limited access from land, or require a run across the bay, weather permitting. (Many boaters and guides won't even fish them, worried about currents conflicting with waves, or losing anchors and tackle. Some even fret about having too many fish to clean at day's end).

Redfish and trout school around the rocks and anglers can catch their limits in the first hour. These areas also get occasional visitors, like snook and tarpon, mostly during August and September. The variety of food and limited fishing pressure allows gamefish to remain around these rocks for prolonged periods. If

you happen to arrive at the jetty during one of those peak periods, you may talk about that day for years to come.

Another reason fishing pressure might be limited is the season. It might be a football weekend in Texas, for instance. During winter, a lot of anglers give up the sport completely for the sake of keeping warm. Jetty fishing in a New England winter means warm clothes and waders—whatever it takes to stay warm and dry. It also means there won't be a lot of fishing pressure. If you decide to go and the fish are biting rapid-fire, you will be the one talking about it around the fireplace that evening.

Docks, Bridges and Piers

Having been a poor boy most of my life, I spent a lot of time fishing off docks, bridges and piers. Like many other types of structures, these areas provided access to good fishing water, and some of the best habitat around. Many areas had lights for night action, that attracted shrimp and small minnows—which in turn attracted larger fish, some of the largest predators around.

During college days, with some free time, I drove to the nearest bridge and spent countless hours fishing, sometimes every night for a straight week. I learned a lot about fishing, caught a lot of great fish, and still fish those same areas to this day.

The lesson here is that certain areas still attract gamefish. It might be some piling that allows fish to rest out of the current—until it decides to chase after food. Or, it might be one spot that has a night light shining down, that draws schools of small baitfish. It takes time to learn these spots, and it's up to you to figure out what it is that draws fish to the spot. Once you know the attraction, it's easier to target gamefish there.

These structures can be found in just about every inshore fishery in the country. They're just as productive in Maine as they are in North Carolina, simply because they provide habitat for marine life. While not every dock, pier or

Hungry snook eyeballs a live pinfish. This is heavier tackle fishing; the snook is fond of diving behind cover, when it feels the hook.

bridge is a fishing wonderland, most of these structures hold their share of fish at one time or another, and it's up to you to figure out where and when fish intend to congregate there.

DOCKS

Many docks hold fish, but the best docks have something different or special that really keep the fish hanging around. For instance, a deep hole at the end of the dock created by the propeller of a boat blowing out sand will draw seatrout and other fish looking for deeper, warmer water in cold weather. A patch of grass along one side of the dock might draw mullet that in turn attract snook. A nearby oyster bar might hold crabs that lure redfish and sheepshead.

Nice shade under the dock means that several species of fish will congregate here.

Some of the best docks to fish have bigger structures on them. Boat houses or roofed areas are designed to protect boats from the sun, but they also provide shade for gamefish looking for shelter during the brightest times of the day. A light down low to the water on that same structure will also draw baitfish at night.

Dilapidated docks that don't see a lot of traffic hold their share of fish as well. With no one to spook the fish off, they can feed around the docks comfortably for several days at a time. These same docks tend to have pilings that have been around for a long time and have lots of marine growth on them, which attracts everything from worms to shrimp and small crabs. These food items draw feeding gamefish.

Even components of the docks themselves

Any time you fish a dock, keep in mind that the structure often attracts predatory fish. They may want shade or a good place to hunt.

can be a draw. In Florida, I find the best red-fish action around docks with PVC pilings, as opposed to standard wood pilings. Oysters and barnacles that attach to PVC are easier for

be on their guard for approaching danger. By wading or fishing out of a boat, you can approach the structure without spooking fish, and still make effective casts close to the dock.

In the open bay, structures like this dock attract a variety of predators.

redfish to pry off—as are the shrimp and crabs that hide in there. Conversely, I find the better snook fishing around wooden docks. These docks usually have more growth and provide more habitat for small shrimp and minnows.

Any time you fish a dock, keep in mind that the structure often attracts predatory fish. They may want shade or might find the pilings a good place to hunt. Species like sheepshead require structure, as it provides the marine growth necessary for their diet. (Where would a sheepshead be without barnacles?) Flounder are notorious for feeding on small minnows attracted to structure. They sit motionless on the bottom where minnows gather, often right beside pilings or seawalls, ambushing baits that pass close overhead.

Under most circumstances, if you're going to fish tight up against a dock, it's best to wade or fish from a boat. The second you step on a dock, it sends vibrations into the water. (Unless you happen to move in a very stealthy manner. Like a Ninja warrior, perhaps; the black robe is optional.) Fish sense these vibrations and will

Tip-toeing on the dock at night helped yield this trophy-size snook.

That being said, a lot of docks extend far out into the bays and backwaters, allowing access to deeper water nearby. In these areas, anglers cast away from the structures and work their baits back in. Some of the best seatrout fishing in Louisiana and Texas takes place at night around lighted docks. The lights draw shrimp, which in turn attract trout. All an angler has to do is pitch out a live shrimp, and wait for a trout to slurp it up. (Some home owners have installed underwater lights, including green lights, for this very purpose. In clear water you can see large predator fish shapes passing over the light, with a circling school of nervous baitfish).

FISH AROUND BRIDGES

Bridges have their own share of different habitats that makes them sure spots to find fish. Combine good habitat with moving water, and you can bet fish are going to feed in the area. Tactics for finding gamefish around bridges start with finding their food source, and then working the edge of that bait. This might be minnows, mullet, bunker or shrimp. It requires patience and concentration to learn these spots, but once you figure them out, you can return for years to come.

Some bridges have fisherman-friendly cat-

Some bridges are quite long, like the Chesapeake Bay Bridge Tunnel. It runs for several miles and then turns into a tunnel for about a mile, and then back into a bridge again. There's a large rest area on the south end of the tunnel, which has a small pier on it. That pier can be a good place to fish, but the adjacent rocks that protect it from the elements really draw a lot of tautog and striped bass.

The first three or four sets of bridge pilings just south off this structure also hold a lot of fish. They're attracted to those nearby rocks, but also feed in the current around the bridge. The fish can move back and forth from one structure to the other with minimal effort, and take advantage of two different types of feeding zones.

walks that provide easy access to the action. Other bridges require a bit more effort to hook and land fish. Anglers have created tools like a bridge gaff or hoop net for landing fish below these structures.

For many nocturnal species, bridges offer attractive lights that pull in the bait. Many aren't really designed for that task. A fair number of bridges are set up for fishing and do have lights designed to shine down on the water. Bridges in the Florida Keys are famous for their night-time fishing activity. Tarpon, big mangrove snapper, permit and other gamefish gather around these bridges to feed on crabs and baitfish caught up in the near-constant

Hooked tarpon tail-walks toward protective bridge span and cover in the Florida Keys.

currents. Daytime boat traffic has forced these fish to become more nocturnal over the years—so some of the best tarpon fishing in the Keys takes place around these bridges after dark.

Some of the best bridge fishing is found around fenders or structures in the middle of the bridge where boats pass. These are usually over the deepest water or main channel. The fenders have a large number of sturdy pilings and are usually marked with lights close to the water. The lights attract bait, while the fenders break the current and attract gamefish. Put the two very close together and it's easy to figure out what happens.

Another thing to keep in mind is that some of the best action around these structures is for smaller food fish like snapper, sheepshead, sandperch and porgies. Though most of these fish average around a pound, they're great fun on light tackle. And it only takes three or four to make a good meal. There are many days when flashy gamefish just aren't biting. The day can be saved by caching ladyfish, jacks and a host of other hard-fighting fish that are willing to bend a rod.

If you're going to fish from any of these structures, be prepared with the right gear. Big fish, like snook and tarpon, know there's safety in those pilings, and that's where they head for, once hooked. They might run for open water early in the fight, but as they get tired and you reel them closer, those line-cutting pilings beneath your feet are going to look

mighty good to a big fish. This is not the place to chase large fish with light tackle. If you're going to target some real brutes, bring out the big guns, and that means heavy tackle that can

Some of the best bridge fishing is four

Shadows play a part in the games gamefish play. During the day, some big fish lurk in the shade, knowing baitfish in the sunlight can't quite see them. At night, gamefish stay just outside the lights, in the darkness, waiting for baitfish, shrimp and crabs to pass by in the lit areas.

stop a big fish cold. If you prefer light-tackle species like pompano or Spanish mackerel, you can make it happen with lighter gear.

pelagic fish such as cobia, king mackerel and big sharks. These same piers have a lot of small food fish around them, for anglers that aren't after big game. That could be any of dozens of

PIER FISHING

Don't underestimate the potential of a small fishing pier, particularly the ones that don't get a lot of fishing pressure. Some of the largest snook I have ever hooked and/or landed in Florida have been off dinky little small-town fishing piers, where I was the only person there.

The best piers are really big ocean or Gulf structures, however. Some piers are over 1,000 feet long, with anglers accessing coastal

Eager anglers work their jigs on Spanish mackerel during winter action in South Florida.

und fenders or structures in the middle of the bridge where boats pass.

coastal species, too numerous to list here.

One of the first things you'll want to learn about fishing any given pier is how to catch bait. If you stick with lures, you won't run into this problem, but you will find that most pier fishermen use bait at some time or another. Many private piers (that charge a very minor day fee) also have small tackle shops that sell

What to Bring

Pier fishing often requires specialized tackle, particularly if you are going to chase the big stuff. Long rods that can increase your casting distance will allow you to reach out and touch some of the species that don't come in tight to the structure. These heavy rods are often designed to cast a weight out from the pier where it can hold bottom and allow the angler to slide a float and bait down the line. Other rods are designed for casting small tandem jigs for Spanish mackerel and pompano. Still others are designed for lobbing heavy plugs at bluefish, stripers and monster reds.

The best way to learn what tackle you'll need is to visit the pier and see what the best pier anglers are using. Like jetty fishermen, hardcore pier anglers are a rather tight-knit group, often called "pier rats." They usually have a serious preference for particular tackle, based on years of experience. Pier rats are a special breed, and take their fishing seriously. Hang around these guys and ask questions when it's appropriate, and you'll learn from them. The rest of your pier fishing knowledge will come from personal experiences, by putting in the hours. SB

frozen bait, but it's hard to beat a freshly caught live bait for vitality.

Bait can arrive in many different forms. At the Lake Worth Pier just south of West Palm Beach, Florida, a live calico crab is the best bait for monster (trophy) permit. That bait has to be caught by using a crab trap lowered off the pier. On some piers off the Virginia coast, a small live bluefish will get munched by a 30-pound redfish. Cut pieces of that bluefish make excellent bait for larger bluefish. So, every pier has its little nuances to be learned, before you can catch fish on a regular basis. Concentrate on learning what the food source is for local gamefish.

Gear for the pier: Above, wheels are nice for carrying a load of ice and fish. Below, hoop net is lowered to land fish far below.

Fishing in the blazing sun on hot planks isn't a requirement. Night-time is often the right time for many of those same fish. A lot of these fish don't even approach piers until after dark. Some of the best weakfish trips I had as a boy were on New Jersey piers after dark, for instance. In those days when weakfish stocks were strong, it was common to catch a handful of fish over 10 pounds in less than an hour of fishing.

Whether you're drawn to docks, bridges or piers, remember it is barnacle-covered structure that draws natural bait and bigger fish and keeps them around. That same structure will also help get you out to the fish. They offer a nice, safe viewpoint where things can be seen from above.

Pier Rats and Pier Fish

Piers are another good source of access to fish. Much like docks and bridges, piers stretch far into open water, often stretching out from shore to deeper water. And, because most piers have lights, they draw fish day and night. In a lot of cases, piers provide the only solid structure in a given area—so they draw immense baitfish schools. The big guys aren't far behind.

Public fishing piers dot the coastline, and those on the beach itself are built to withstand some serious storms. Modern piers are built with concrete high above the water, often with removable deck boards. They're safe, offer a good view of the water below, and should not be overlooked as a source of fishing pleasure. Often they yield the best fishing action for an entire region.

Many inshore (bay) fishing piers are small public structures that can be fished for free. The thing to remember is that many of these structures get a lot of fishing pressure, so a lot of the best fish aren't exactly where anglers think they should be. The end of the pier may hold deeper water and mud bottom, which turns to sand halfway back to shore. Flounder normally prefer the mud, but heavy fishing pressure might mean the largest fish still left are lying up around the first few pilings in much more shallow water. SB

Happy pier rat (pier veteran) with yet another Spanish mackerel. This guy is well on his way to catching a daily bag limit during the winter run in South Florida.

Spillway Fishing

These days, water management is big business in just about every state, and when man decides to control the water flow, there's bound to be spillways involved. These spillways provide a dam to control water on one side of the structure, but can also be lowered to allow water to flow to the other side of the structure. Because there's a large volume of water being moved from one area to another,

In many cases, the best fishing around spillways is not in the direct flow of water, but on the edges of moving water.

fish are going to get mixed up in the move. When baitfish are displaced they get disoriented and when that happens, they get eaten.

Spillways are built in all shapes and sizes, from small dikes to large river locks capable of holding large boats and even barges. In each case, it's the movement of water and a food source that make these areas so hot with action. I've seen days when water was flowing over a spillway, carrying so much bait that fish were literally jumping out of the water in one big feeding frenzy, just below the dam. I've seen anglers catch snook on every cast for an hour, with tarpon facing into the moving current, blasting everything that came by.

In many cases, the best fishing around spillways is not in the direct flow of water, but on the edges of moving water, where eddies boil and spin. Baitfish are usually worn out from the heavy currents of moving water, even addled after going over a spillway, easy targets for predators.

Spillway fishing is best when water is moving, so the time to fish these structures is after the rainy season. The rest of the year these

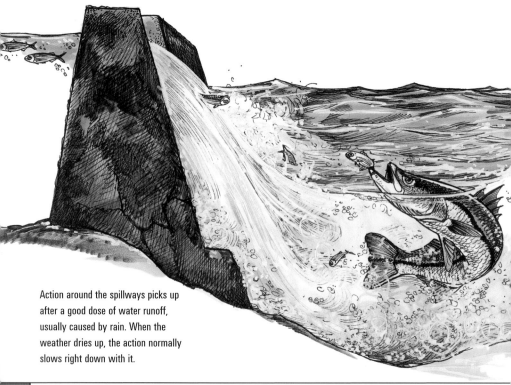

Action around the spillways picks up after a good dose of water runoff, usually caused by rain. When the weather dries up, the action normally slows right down with it.

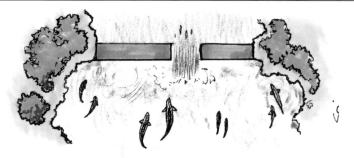
Spillway diagram shows fish resting to each side of the main current flow. Active fish can feed in the middle.

structures do hold fish, but you won't find the big feeding sprees.

The best spillway fishing often takes place the first few days after the spillway is open, when the largest volumes of new water arrive. Baitfish that have been stacked against the upcurrent side get pulled over with the moving water. These small fish generally get swept over during the first four or five days, so timing your trip can be critical. The amount of food flowing over the structure typically declines after a few days, as remaining baitfish in the area escape the water's pull. After several days of water flow, water below the structure may lose a lot of salinity, forcing some gamefish species to retreat downriver. In either case, the best fishing tends to take place right after heavy rains when the water flows best.

Because there is a strong water flow, effective lures and baits can be fairly large. A Red Tail Hawk jig meant for big snook can weigh two ounces or more. Some of the big diving plugs used on stripers can even weigh four or five ounces. These big lures require rods with heavy actions and line capable of landing big

fish. Braided lines with thin diameters (that don't drag in the current) work very well here, though most anglers still use monofilament.

There's also structure to keep in mind when selecting line. Many spillways have nearby structures that fish may use to break that line. Heavy line can stop big fish from reaching structure and increase the odds of landing a trophy. It might not be as sporty as light tackle, but the challenge of stopping a fish over 30 pounds can be just as great.

Not all spillways are large, of course. If you travel around South Florida, you're sure to see some of the flap gates and flood gates along Alligator Alley, the road from Miami to Tampa. This east/west highway is blanketed with roadside canals that drain the Everglades water basin out to sea. Saltwater gamefish move along the entire stretch during the dry season. These little spillway gates flush just enough food and water into new areas to hold good numbers of gamefish. Anglers have caught snook and tarpon on every cast for hours at a time along these structures. Sometimes, schools of finger mullet are so thick, the snook were literally leaping out of the water, blasting them.

Around these little structures (really just a pipe or two), light tackle or even fly tackle is appropriate. When geared to the size of the fish and the lack of threatening structure, these openwater areas are superb fishing arenas. Just watch out for alligators that can steal your catch. They don't call it Alligator Alley for nothing.

As with other areas of structure, don't overlook night fishing opportunities. Many gamefish are nocturnal feeders, particularly during summer. Baitfish also stack up in the dark as they utilize their large numbers to avoid predation. Big schools of bait often mean consistent feeding sprees—when fish are blasting baits at night, action can be fast and furious.

Overall, spillways present a unique challenge for shorebound anglers, allowing access to outstanding fishing. They should not be overlooked, as you develop your inshore fishing skills.

What to Bring

The rule of thumb for spillway fishing is to use the lightest tackle you can get away with, and still land fish. This will allow your lures and baits to act more natural in the current. If your bait doesn't swim with a natural motion, you're defeating the cause, because a fish will never eat it.

Just because fishing is best at spillways when water is flowing over with some force, don't overlook your chances with a light current flow. Any water flowing over the spillway will likely pull some small fish over with it, and gamefish will be there. That might mean they're smaller, but the fishing can be fun. When the water is flowing lightly, fish will usually move up close, with some fish holding against the wall of the weir itself. That's the time when light tackle and small lures or baits can produce great results.

A finger mullet allowed to swim into a corner or against the wall of the weir has no avenue of escaping from attacking snook, jacks or redfish. A shrimp in the same situation is dead meat for just about any gamefish. Small jigs often used in tandem are deadly.

Working the spillway current. Very often the action turns on at sunrise and sunset. At right, one of many spillway snook landed in a boiling current. Below, a variety of hot plastic lures will work here, some better than others, according to what mood the fish are in.

Canals and Creeks

Backwater creeks, canals and finger channels represent some of the most diverse fishing terrain found in inshore waters. From narrow oil and gas pipeline canals cutting through the marshes of Louisiana and Texas, to finger channels built for boater access in Florida's many waterfront developments, these areas are small highways for inshore gamefish. Most canals are tidally driven, with marine fish using them to move from one area to another. They often duck into these creeks or canals as sanctuary when water levels drop, then move back to the shallows with the rising tide.

These narrow waterbodies also offer a variety of different structures, such as dropoffs, old docks and pilings, deeper holes, corner eddies, smaller cuts with advanced tidal flow and mangrove-covered shorelines. Many of these areas are off the beaten path, sometimes "way back in the swamp." Fish that move in there often stay for prolonged periods and get used to feeding in one area. That makes them more susceptible to being caught.

A lot of these small canals hold some nice fish, even huge ones. A prime example are South Florida canals, home to tarpon exceeding 100 pounds. A creek or canal barely wide enough to allow two boats to pass may hold the fish of a lifetime. Most home owners on the water don't even suspect this; many don't even fish. These canals can be explored with a quiet trolling motor, since tidal water isn't closed to

Fish that move in there often stay for prolonged periods and get used to feeding in one area. That makes them more susceptible to being caught.

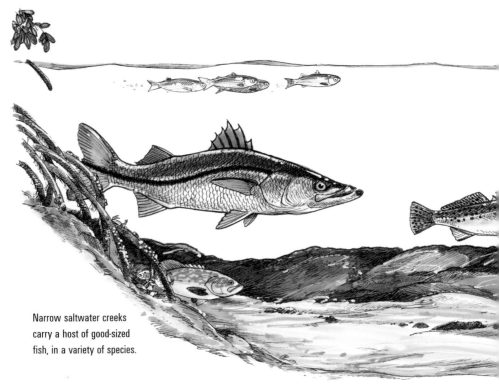

Narrow saltwater creeks
carry a host of good-sized
fish, in a variety of species.

Exploring the secrets of a tidal creek. Is there a trophy fish around the next bend?

the public. Discouraged perhaps, in some areas, but still generally allowed. These quiet backwaters, far from any marine predators, are havens for older fish tired of fighting the tides. In Texas, the annual winning sheepshead in their state-wide, summer-long tournament, good for winning a new boat, is very often caught in a canal in some subdivision, some crusty 10-pounder that gave up the jetty currents for a

quieter retirement. Huge trout have been seen in there, as well. Folks with canals behind their homes are fond of putting out night lights, either above or below the surface, to attract fish. Baitfish and shrimp wander through the lights and get nabbed. The bottom lights in clear water are impressive; you can see a ball of baitfish milling above the light, with much larger shapes (trout and redfish) passing by.

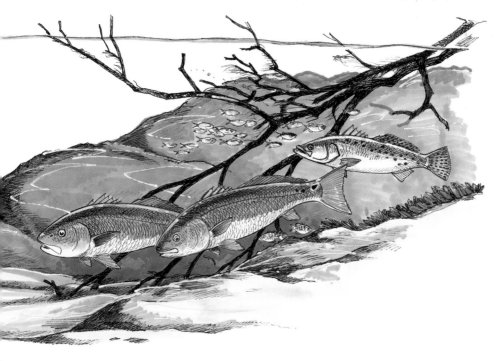

The same qualities that attract gamefish to canals attract baitfish. These quiet, protected waters with little tidal current are havens for bait.

South Florida canals with their lights are of course more apt to be populated by nocturnal snook and tarpon, both of which can feed at night and sleep during the day.

Some of the larger canals can be quite deep. These canals are great for trolling up and

Texas are brimming with these baits at night, and it's a simple task to catch a few pounds with a castnet. Though small, they're great for chum later on.

Because most canals and finger channels are deep, they're outstanding cold-weather areas

Peaceful scene fishing in an isolated saltwater creek. It's possible to have such remote spots all to yourself.

down, with lipped plugs. A powerful electric motor, able to move the boat along at trolling speed, makes the quiet approach even more effective. The fish here generally are not as scared of outboard motor noise, because they get used to normal daily boat traffic. Just ease along up one canal and down another, until a fish is hooked. Then cut the motor and fight the fish in a normal fashion.

The same qualities that attract gamefish to canals and creeks attract baitfish. These quiet, protected waters (very quiet on weekdays) with little tidal current are havens for schooling juvenile bait. Thick schools of small menhaden love these canals; canals in Louisiana and East

to fish. They attract a host of fish during winter, when plunging air temperatures force them to look hastily for deeper water. On those nights when temperatures drop, fish move to the bottom to stay warm, with every foot of extra water above them acting as a security blanket. The lack of breaking waves in these canals no doubt helps prevent mixing of colder water above. The next day, if the sun is out, fish can rise near the surface to soak up any faint rise in water temperature. These fish generally stay in the sheltered spots like this until cold weather abates, with the wind direction switching to the east or hopefully south. Then, like some signal, they all leave together. Witnesses at night in Texas have seen a parade of fish leaving these cold-weather sanctuaries, with a complete mix of species passing by—black drum, big mullet, redfish, sheepshead and trout all swimming side-by-side in a river of passing traffic. When it's time to go, and disperse back in the deeper bays, these fish know it.

Sheltered canals behind waterfront homes offer sanctuary to some large fish.

FL 4039 JY

Perhaps they know they shouldn't stay long, cramped up in close quarters, for too long. That cold-water sanctuary may represent a trap after too long. Certainly, many anglers have descended on the coast during these cold weather snaps, anchoring sometimes hundreds of boats above fish hiding from the cold. The harvest in years past, when there were no bag limits, was pretty fearsome, with some boats keeping hundreds of redfish alone. Many fish were even snagged. In South Texas, where water depths are especially shallow, any canal or marina with eight feet of water became a sanctuary for desperate winter fish. The crowd of "snaggers," as they're sometimes called, arriving from up to a hundred miles away, had no problem catching or snagging a car trunk full of eight-pound and bigger trout. It was a sad ending for these trophy-size fish.

Many of these winter fish also dive into the Intracoastal Waterway when cold weather arrives. Very likely this canal has saved millions from freezing. The only downside is that tugboats pushing barges up and down the canal are said to churn up a lot of gamefish with their huge propellers. They also mix water temperature layers like a giant kitchen blender. In years past there has been an outcry from fishermen who want the Intracoastal Waterway closed to barge traffic during a severe freeze. Whether interstate commerce will take a backseat to gamefish populations remains to be seen. SB

Tight Quarters

Any time you have an abundance of food in tight quarters, predators may take advantage. When mullet get bottled up in a creek or canal by bigger fish, the action can be ferocious.

Some of the best structures to fish here are seawalls, which provide a natural barrier

Mullet blasted from the water along the seawall. Looks like the work of jacks.

against escape. Gamefish push small baitfish up against these walls, pinning them down for destruction. Jack crevalle are especially famous for seawall hunting; Florida residents with backyard canals can tell stories of watching jacks blow baitfish out of the water, often bouncing them off hard objects.

CHAPTER 5

How Fish Really Think

There are certain things that motivate us. Urges like hunger, comfort and reproduction build the habits of our everyday lives. Fish are no different. They have needs on a more visceral level, but those needs are motivations for their actions.

Food is the primary motivation of all fish. And a full belly will certainly help it feel more comfortable. If a fish can find a place where it can eat well, it will generally hang around for more easy meals. If that place offers a desirable temperature and fulfills its visual needs, then so much the better. On the other hand, if that fish is near freezing, it may sacrifice an easy meal for warmer climate.

Reproduction is a major force that concentrates fish in one location. The fish may be there to propagate, yet they must eat during that time. And, the more fish in an area, the greater the competition for food. By understanding what motivates fish you can determine the basis of their habits, and use this knowledge to improve your catch rate. Let's explore some of the basic motivations for all inshore gamefish species.

Fish move from zone to zone, seeking better conditions. When they find it, they stay until conditions change.

Seeking the comfort zone. This tarpon is gulping air, to make up for low oxygen content in the water during hot weather in summer.

Get Into Their Comfort Zone

I f you really want to catch more fish, you need to understand what their motivations are. Even on a good day, a fish has a brain the size of a pea, so it only gravitates toward certain things, with comfort being a key motivator. Like any animal, fish are more relaxed in their comfort zone. That means they're more likely to follow other motivations—like eating.

Comfort can be an ambiguous word. In many cases, comfort means a fish is in a temperature zone that is optimal for feeding, spawning and protective activities. That doesn't exactly happen all the time; many fish have small preferred temperature ranges, and during different seasons, the air and water temperatures swing back and forth.

During summer, the coolest period of the day is just before dawn. The land and water have cooled overnight, and the air temperature is lowest just before sunrise. Fish that enjoy warm climates but not extremely hot weather—like spotted seatrout—are more likely to be active in summer in the morning (if the tide is moving). Fish that prefer hot weather, like permit, will be more active when the sun comes up, and get even friskier as the day wears on and the sun warms up the flats.

Other fish like Spanish mackerel prefer cool water from 68 to 74 degrees, and will move as those temperatures change. A bluefish in its comfort zone is going to be a lot more aggressive and stronger than a bluefish in water that is too warm. Every fish species has a different temperature and comfort range. Learn those temperatures and how they relate to different fish, and you narrow down the search for them.

Another factor of comfort is safety. If a fish doesn't feel safe, it's not going to actively feed, much less in a reckless fashion. Reckless feeding sprees often produce outstanding catches, of course, and I say bring them on. I want those fish to feed without a care, which certainly helps my odds of catching. Reckless is good.

So, when fish feel safe in their optimum temperature range, the next factor they consider is finding food. Like any animal, fish have to eat. It's a major motivation, though comfort usually comes first. Some fish require nourishment a lot more often than other species. Free-swimming, coastal pelagics like bluefish move around more often than some, so they burn a lot of energy and need a steady source of food. Fish that remain still for long periods, on the other hand, can go for greater lengths without eating, because they

Comfort means temperatures optimal for feeding, spawning and protection.

Catching a fish at mid-day. Opposite, a snook has it made in the shade, far away from human activity.

don't burn up the calories.

What a fish eats also determines how often it needs to feed. The higher the fat and oil content of its prey, the more energy produced and the less often it needs to eat. The same goes for the size of its prey. If a spotted seatrout eats a

ture. Shrimp make their runs during optimum water temperatures, and many mass baitfish movements like the annual mullet runs are motivated by a change in seasons. Mullet and flounder both migrate into the Gulf of Mexico, moving through the passes in major numbers

A steady food source is often related to comfort and water temperature. Few gamefish abandon a good food source.

14-inch mullet, it won't have to feed again for several days. If that same trout eats only a shrimp, it will continue to feed.

The thing to look for in your favorite fish is the best available food source. Very few gamefish will abandon a good food source, unless they're threatened or made uncomfortable by water conditions. Since fish don't have eyelids, the sun can be a factor causing fish to temporarily move. If there's a solid food source, fish are more likely to ignore bright sunlight and feed until full, then move off into deeper water where the light doesn't penetrate as much.

A steady food source is often related to comfort and tempera-

every November, when those first strong cold fronts arrive. Wind direction can also play a key role, but temperature is the greater factor. During bait migrations you can expect gamefish

Natural Order of Things

From the minute a fish is born until the day it dies, there is some predator willing to eat it. That means every fish has to be on its guard at all times. Predators come in many forms, too: It might be a larger fish, a bird like an osprey or blue heron, even crustaceans like the mantis shrimp, preying on juvenile fish. There's a host of predators out there, and as a fish ages it learns what to avoid and when to be on guard. Without a doubt, anything six feet tall approaching a 24-inch fish is going to put that fish in a wary mode.

Because of the threat of predation, one of nature's ways to make fish feel safer is to bring them together in large numbers. Schooling fish represent more eyes to watch for predators, and a bigger target that can be intimidating to smaller or juvenile predators. It's common to think of baitfish gathering in huge schools to avoid predation, but other species follow this same pattern. Off the southeast coast, even mature jack crevalle gather in large schools for protection. Permit, striped bass, bluefish, Spanish mackerel—all do the same thing. They school for safety, feeding, even spawning.

Schooling mullet are one of the most important food sources for gamefish.

Big mullet fulfills its obligation to feed other predators, though in this case it's an osprey that snatched it from shallow water.

that don't mind similar water temperatures to be there—they just can't help those easy meals.

Once fish do actively feed, they will generally let down their guard and are certainly more susceptible to being caught on hook and line. Feeding fish are on a roll, less likely to spook from a tackle box slamming or an approaching angler. Use those feeding frenzies to your advantage, because they don't happen all the time. More often fish have to work hard to find their meals, making them hard to approach and fool.

Anglers often say fish are smart, but I don't believe it. Fish have excellent senses and often detect approaching anglers, and can sense a threat. Their thought patterns (the fish) focus on comfort, safety, food and spawning and those items are the four major motivators for all fish species.

If that is the case, as anglers we should utilize that knowledge. We need to learn the favored temperatures for gamefish in our areas. Every state is different; seatrout in Texas feed actively in 70-degree water, while the same species in Florida likes it above 72 degrees. (Actually they're a subspecies; Florida trout have a lot more spots, while Texas trout often have a purple hue on their backs). Striped bass in North Carolina favor water in the low 60s, while the same species in New York favor water in the mid-50s.

Spawning Fish

Spawning behavior certainly brings fish together. Any time you bring a large number of gamefish to one spot, you increase the odds of catching fish, because they get competitive. If there are several hundred fish in one spot and only a limited amount of food, they become aggressive. If they don't, they go hungry. Spawning activity also makes them burn calories, which makes them hungry.

A school of hungry fish all bunched up in one location will feed with reckless abandon when the time is right. It might mean the fish will feed on a certain tide or at night, but they have to eat. Each species has a specific feeding pattern for spawning, and it's important to learn that pattern so you can target fish easier. If they feed at night, that's the time to fish for them. Most often the feeding patterns are related to when the local food source is most available. Shrimp and crabs run on the outgoing tide, so that's the best time for tarpon and striped bass to eat them.

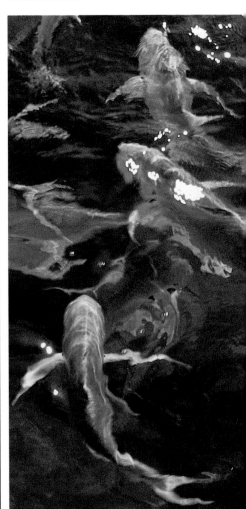

To be consistent, learn those optimum water temperatures. Many anglers can do so simply by touch. Sticking your hand in the water reveals it's not too cold and fish are likely to be feeding. Of course, a temperature gauge on the boat is more accurate. Look where a fish feels safest. Then move on to where food is in the area. Spawning behavior is typically seasonal, and very consistent.

Try to find the most consistent areas to fish that offer the best scenarios for all four factors, and you will likely catch a lot more fish. Even just one of those factors can swing the odds in your favor. SB

A horde of hungry jack crevalle schooling together for safety and perhaps spawning duties. In either case, they're usually hungry and not shy. Above, a nice striped bass plucked from a feeding school.

CHAPTER 6

Favorite Inshore Species

I f you dedicate any amount of time to inshore fishing, you're sure to develop a favorite target species. You might like its abundance or its power and speed. Some favor acrobatic gamefish, while other anglers prefer aggressiveness. Some popular gamefish aren't even considered good table fare, but put up such a fight that the angler is often left guessing if he's really in the game.

Whatever your favorite inshore fish to target, you're sure to encounter others who share a similar passion for finding and catching that gamefish. Some species have anglers so enamored with their fighting or food qualities, anglers become borderline cultists. Whether you're a hardcore fisherman or just an occasional weekender, the specific fish you target will give direction and focus to your fishing tackle and techniques.

The more you can learn about the species you want to catch, the easier it is to understand their actions, and to plan your fishing trips to take advantage of that. And, for more information on these gamefish, be sure to check out *Sport Fish of Florida*, *Sport Fish of the Gulf of Mexico* and *Sport Fish of the Atlantic*.

Getting to know some of the finest coastal sport fish on the planet.

See DVD for more on your favorite species.

Fine seatrout taken while wading East Matagorda Bay on the Texas coast. Below, jetty redfish caught on the Florida-Georgia border at Fernandina.

The Best of the Best

If you're going to dedicate serious fishing time to inshore waters, you might as well learn some of the characteristics of the species you're after. In the following pages are some of the most pursued of inshore gamefish, along with my personal favorite baits and fishing locations for finding and catching these fish. Keep in mind these are only my personal opinions. If you really want to learn more about all the gamefish species found in your local inshore waters, be sure to check out these other books from the *Sportsman's Best Series*: *Sport Fish of Florida; Sport Fish of the Atlantic*, and *Sport Fish of the Gulf of Mexico*.

Tightening the drag
finally turned this
speedy bonefish around.

STRIPED BASS

Choice Location: Stripers have a very broad range in the mid and upper Atlantic, and they're well known for chasing baitfish schools up into the bays and sounds, but if you really want to catch striped bass, you'll be best served fishing the beaches. Concentrate on areas with a deep trough running close to shore. These fish like to feed in five to 10 feet of water.

Choice Baits: Although they eat a variety of live baits from bunker to eels, if you're going to fish the surf, try working a 2- to 4-ounce swimming plug. Work it through the breaking waves and foamy whitewater, where these fish can really zero in on it.

Striped bass have been called the white-tailed deer of inshore waters, because they eat everything.

BLUEFISH

Choice Location: Bluefish range from Florida through the upper Atlantic, but you really need to be in their northern range to catch the largest fish (over 15 pounds) with any frequency. You'll notice most bluefish schools carry fish of the same size, because the species is so cannibalistic. If you want to target jumbo blues, you need to fish beaches and inlets in the northeast states. Concentrate on areas with good water depth, at least six feet or more. Great action can often be found in about 25 feet of water.

Choice Baits: Bluefish are voracious feeders that will consume just about anything smaller that wanders in front of them. When they're schooling, they get even more confident and aggressive. It's a real blast to cast big surface poppers and watch them crush the lures on top. Given a choice, however, I'll take a silver spoon over just about anything when after bluefish. The flash of the spoon and its slow, wobbling motion really draw these gamefish.

Huge, trophy-size bluefish. These guys get mean on baitfish.

WEAKFISH

Choice Location: I've caught weakfish from Florida to New York, but the best concentrations of these gamefish occur in the bays and sounds of the northeastern Atlantic states, from Chesapeake Bay to Long Island Sound. Find a good deep hole bordering a sandbar or expanse of flats and moving water, and you have the recipe for good weakfish action. Look for good action at night as well, under lighted bridges and piers.

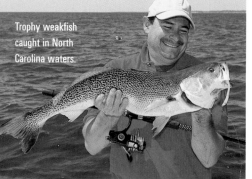

Trophy weakfish caught in North Carolina waters.

Choice Baits: Like other members of the croaker family, weakfish eat anything from worms to shrimp and finfish. Given a choice, they want the largest bait they can find, and that usually means a good-size bunker or croaker. For me, the fun in catching weakies is bouncing a bucktail or soft plastic jig along the upcurrent side of a bar and letting it fall into a deep hole, where these fish will 'thump" the lure with authority.

BLACK DRUM

Choice Location: Though small "puppy" drum provide good sport and food on the table, it is the massive adult drum that may be the biggest fish many folks ever catch in inshore waters. Popular from Virginia to Texas, this fish is widespread. They're really attracted to healthy oyster reefs in 12 to 20 feet of water, but they may turn up anywhere, even offshore around oil platforms in 40 to 100 feet of water.

Choice Baits: Their back teeth, called pharyngeal teeth, are built for crushing and grinding, so it's no surprise that shellfish and clams are a favorite prey of drum. Don't waste your time fishing for these guys with fish as bait; best items are chunks of blue crab and whole shrimp. During the popular "drum run" each March, big spawners up to 70 pounds cruise within reach of jetties and seawalls near deeper water, and that's when folks show up with heavier tackle and blue crabs as bait.

REDFISH

Choice Location: If you fish coastal waters from Texas to Maryland, you're familiar with red drum. You probably believe your waters have the best fishing in the country. The largest fish lurk off the Carolinas. The Mosquito Lagoon in Titusville has huge schools of fish in shallow water, which is a rare treat to see. If you really want to have fun catching redfish, you should concentrate on their entire local range. Fish those schools of keeper-size fish in one to three feet of water, then try catching a trophy off a jetty or beachfront. For me, sight-fishing a school of tailing reds working over a shallow grass bottom is as good as it gets. It's a classic sight, one that coastal artists love to paint.

Choice Baits: The downward-pointing mouth of a redfish makes it difficult for these fish to catch topwater baits. That's why it's better to concentrate on using lures and baits that work below the surface or near bottom. Redfish eat shrimp and crabs with vigor, but really love finfish. That's why a gold spoon is my first choice when chasing these fish.

FLOUNDER

Choice Location: "Okay, so this guy's a loser?" Far from it. Flounder are one of those fish that cover the entire range of inshore waters, and they're just as fun to catch as they are to eat. Action is usually seasonal, but very dependable throughout their wide range. It's more important to list their favorite bottom feature here, which is over sand or mud bottom in two to eight feet of water. Flounder really orient to structure that forms a break in the current, where they can find small minnows and other food attracted to the same areas as habitat.

Choice Baits: Juvenile mullet are one of the top flounder baits, but they'll eat everything from shrimp to bloodworms and even mature bunker, depending on the flounder's size. Soft plastic jigs and even cut strips of flounder belly catch an awful lot of flounder as well, but for day-in, day-out flounder pounding it's hard to beat a live killifish (mud minnow) suspended just off the bottom with a slip-sinker rig. Mud minnows are tougher than any other live bait, and work harder for you while on the hook.

Rough-and-tumble redfish fights against a shallow-running plug. Redfish are truly loved by countless coastal fishermen.

SPOTTED SEATROUT

Choice Location: From Texas to Virginia, spotted seatrout have found a place in the hearts of a huge number of inshore anglers. On the Gulf Coast they roam the beaches and have even been caught around wrecks and oil platforms 20 miles offshore in 45 feet of water. On the Atlantic Coast they're more often found in shallow bays and estuaries. If you want consistency with your seatrout catches, then look for the fish in two to four feet of water over patchy grassflats with sand, mud or shell holes.

Choice Baits: Shrimp are the main diet for seatrout all along the coast, but their focus on shrimp can be seasonal. Mullet and other finfish, like piggy perch, croakers, pigfish and bunker can really catch a lot of nice trout, as will lures that imitate these species—particularly soft plastic jigs, jerkbaits and topwater plugs. However, if it's consistency we're looking for from seatrout, you'd be hard pressed to beat a live shrimp suspended under a popping cork.

PERMIT

Choice Location: Many anglers don't realize that permit range well up the Florida Gulf and Atlantic coasts, with big schools migrating out to the offshore wrecks during late spring. Still, if you want the ultimate thrill of stalking and catching a permit, you should do so over shallow grassflats of South Miami and the Florida Keys.

Choice Baits: Permit are primarily crustacean eaters, although I have caught them on live finger mullet. A big shrimp placed in front of a spawning aggregation is sure to get lunched. I've even caught a good number of juvenile permit in the surf while using sandfleas for bait. If you're going to pursue these strong, inshore gamefish, you might as well offer them the best bait possible, and that's a live dollar-sized crab. (That's a silver dollar, not a paper dollar). Cast the crab in front of a cruising permit or perhaps one bobbing its tail in the grass, and that crab very likely has a short lease on life.

Nice permit caught off the beach near Stuart, Florida. These fish will do anything for a small, blue crab.

Exotic-looking snook favor tropical waters and more southern latitudes, and don't do well in cold weather.

SNOOK

Choice Location: The structure-oriented habits of snook make this Florida and far-South Texas specialty great targets for anglers who stalk them around inshore bridges, docks and mangrove-lined shores. During summer these fish migrate out to the inlets or prowl the beachfront. In winter they move to deep inshore holes or farther out to nearshore reefs. When these fish aren't spawning or looking for a place to hide from the cold, you can find them most often in two to four feet of water, hunting around sandy holes in the grass flats. In the shallows, snook can be super-aggressive during warm weather. There's nothing like watching a snook blow up a topwater plug or a live bait on the flats.

Choice Baits: Like tarpon, snook have a large diet selection. In winter and spring when the shrimp are running, you can't keep a hungry snook off your bait. During fall when the mullet run, snook show these baitfish schools little or no mercy. That's when soft plastic shrimp imitations and large topwater plugs will catch you a lot of fish. When snook are schooled up, just about any form of live whitebait (pilchards, sardines and threadfin herring) are snook candy. Probably no lure or bait has caught more snook than the Red Tail Hawk jig, however. This white or chartreuse jig with a red trailer is the snook bomb. It's a lure all snook fishermen should have in their tackle boxes.

TARPON

Choice Location: Inshore anglers pursue tarpon from Texas to North Carolina, but Florida has the most consistent tarpon action because of its climate. In the Sunshine State, you can catch tarpon of all sizes in rivers and estuaries or along the beaches. Action is consistent during spring, summer and fall, but for all around consistency try the flats from the Keys to Florida Bay. Here the fish move in dense schools where they can be targeted with fly, lures or bait.

Choice Baits: Tarpon can be incredibly picky, or they can be swimming garbage cans. They'll eat just about anything from shrimp and crabs to live or dead bait-fish, even cleaning-table carcasses. Fly fishing is very effective for tarpon because the fly can be paused in front of the fish for long periods. Whatever natural bait is running the tide in large numbers, at the moment, becomes first on the menu. Many people don't realize that tarpon are adaptable scavengers, and prior to the mid-1960s most anglers pursued the silver king with dead mullet on the bottom. That's still a deadly technique for tarpon of almost all sizes.

BONEFISH

Choice Location: Since bonefish are limited in their range to South Florida and tropical countries, that's where you'll want to hunt for them. This jittery fish has long been one of the most targeted inshore gamefish in Florida, and the big schools of tailing fish in less than a foot of water aren't nearly as accommodating as they once were. Nowadays, the schools are super spooky and hard to target with any regularity. In Florida, catching a bonefish by sight-casting to tailing fish is now an angling accomplishment. The best place to catch bones is in Biscayne Bay and the Florida Keys in two to four feet of water, over a thick grass bottom with a good sandy area nearby. Schools in this situation feed more aggressively, are less likely to spook and can be sight cast to, just like the tailers.

Choice Baits: Most of the food that bonefish ingest is really tiny, mostly small worms, crabs, shrimp and other items that go unnoticed on the flats. Small skimmer-type jigs are deadly on bones, especially when tipped with a bit of shrimp for added scent.

Bones really love eating flies. Or they do at first, anyway, before feeling that tiny hook. Bigger bones love a fat little crab, but shrimp is the food that really pulls the bonefish in close and makes them concentrate on eating, rather than fretting about some nearby boat.

SPANISH MACKEREL

Choice Location: Spanish mackerel are pelagic in nature, which means they're free-swimming and always on the move. The largest schools are found off the beaches of both coasts, and these fish regularly move into inshore waters to chase bait. Given a choice, I fish the big schools of Spanish that congregate in 15 to 35 feet of water along the beaches. These schools hold some of the largest fish and the competition for food among several thousand of these speedy torpedoes makes them more aggressive.

Choice Baits: These fish are picky about what they eat. Shrimp are a mainstay of their diet in the Gulf and Atlantic, but the majority of what they eat is juvenile baitfish and minnows. Given that tidbit of information, you can really beat up on schools of Spanish with jigs, shrimp or just about any small live baitfish. For consistency and sheer action, my preference is to throw silver spoons at the fish and watch them slash at the lure several times until the hook finds a home.

String of Spanish mackerel caught while walking the jetty at Sabine Pass, Texas.

SHEEPSHEAD

Choice Location: These striped bandits are champion bait stealers that are extremely structure-oriented. Just about any branch or tree in the water will attract sheepshead, as will channel markers, rockpiles, seawalls and docks. Sheepshead like to feed in four to 10 feet of water, and the barnacles and oysters coating bridge pilings are where you'll really have success with this species.

Choice Baits: These fish are hardcore crustacean and mollusk eaters, so you might want to focus on what they really eat. Sure, sheepshead will occasionally grab a jig or fly, but they also possess outstanding vision and smell, so if your offering doesn't seem like the real deal, they're going to lose interest. Live fiddler crabs are one of the deadliest sheepshead baits, but a live shrimp is the one offering a sheepshead can't refuse.

Big sheepshead searches hard growth, looking for a meal. These fish usually stay close to structure.

LADYFISH

Choice Location: I often find the biggest ladyfish along the beaches, but also catch them on the flats and in deep holes. They have a range similar to jack crevalle, preferring warm-water climates. At times, ladyfish may locate a hole or dropoff and stack up there in impressive numbers—so that an angler hooks these fish on every cast.

While canals and rivers hold great numbers of these fish, I prefer chasing them in two to five feet of water over large open-water expanses such as over grass flats or around spoil banks.

Choice Baits: Live shrimp are ladyfish killers. The speed and directional changes of ladyfish make them exceptionally good hunters and just about any small baitfish can fall prey. Ladyfish are drawn to concentrations of minnows, shrimp or mullet, but give me a light rod and a soft-bodied or bucktail jig that I can work fast and I'm in ladyfish heaven. Since ladyfish aren't a great food source, be sure to bend the barbs down to make hook removal easy.

CROAKER

Choice Location: If you spend any time fishing inshore waters you're sure to catch more than your share of croakers. There are several species. Most

spend time in inshore bays, and some time along the beach. As a rule, the largest fish are those that move inside the bay to spawn, and those fat croakers are the ones I really love to catch. Big yellowtail

Atlantic croakers find a good deep hole in eight to 15 feet of water to school up during the fall, and when they're ganged up the fishing can be as fun as for anything else.

Croakers off the Louisiana coast around the oil rigs sometimes average two pounds and more.

Choice Baits: The mouth of a croaker faces downward just like a redfish, making them little swimming vacuum cleaners. Sandfleas, shrimp, small crabs, worms and minnows top the list of their favorite food. In the surf, it's hard to beat a live sandflea, which can also catch a lot of other quality fish. Given a choice, I want to fish a live or dead shrimp on a 1/4- to 3/8-ounce leadhead jig, so the bait goes deep quickly.

WHITING

Choice Location: Whether in the surf or inshore waters, whiting are aggressive sight feeders that focus on food very close to shore, sometimes only feet away. Probably the most consistent location to find whiting is in the trough at your local beach, where these small fish ease along the dropoff, hunting for food swept back into the surf with each receding wave. In clear water, whiting roam the beaches in two to six feet of water, where they can be sight-cast to with great success.

Choice Baits: Whiting love everything from small strips of squid to glass minnows and sandfleas. They're sight feeders that attack anything small enough near the bottom. Fresh pieces of shrimp fished in the surf are one of the top baits, but my favorite way to catch whiting is to don a

pair of good polarized sunglasses and walk the beach looking for them, casting a 1/8-ounce white or yellow jig. Bounce the jig off the bottom so that it makes little puffs in the sand, and the whiting will race to grab it. They also fight well, for their size.

A pair of whiting from the surf. These fish are accommodating, fight hard for their size and are good to eat. Popular with the fishing public, too.

JACK CREVALLE

Choice Location: Another wide-ranging gamefish that can be found from Texas through the mid-Atlantic states, the jack roams in all sizes from one-pound rod benders to 40-pound back breakers. These very strong gamefish migrate along Gulf and Atlantic beaches, following any food source in inshore waters and well up into low-salinity areas. I love to catch jacks on the grass-flats and off the beach when the bait is running. And because I'm into the visual aspects of these bruisers, it's great watching a big jack knock bait against a seawall in three to 10 feet of water.

Choice Baits: Smaller jacks will eat just about anything, but larger fish want something substantial in their diets. Still, shrimp and small baitfish have caught more than their share of jacks. And top-water lures, fly poppers and jigs are deadly offerings. Heave an 8- to 12-inch live mullet near a seawall, and you can bet there's going to be a display of eva-sive action, as that bait tries to elude the wrath of a hungry jack crevalle.

Trophy jack crevalle landed after a very hard battle.

POMPANO

Choice Location: The migratory nature of pompano means they're always on the move and cover a lot of different terrain. They run Gulf and Atlantic beaches and regularly move inside inlets to feed in the bays. Inside, they focus on shallow flats and the edges of sandbars in three to five feet of water, often swimming along channel edges on the moving tides. Given a choice, I would rather catch them in the surf, casting off the beach into the trough in four to 10 feet of water, or onto the outside edge of a sandbar.

Choice Baits: Pompano have a keen sense of smell, and can be chummed to a location using sandfleas or shrimp, but because they feed in areas with strong tides, that method can be difficult. Once they locate an area to feed in, they rely on their keen eyesight to catch shrimp, crabs and small clams, and sometimes minnows or small bait-fish. For the most part, pompano are crustacean eaters, and if you're going to target them on a regular basis, then expect to spend a lot of time baiting your hooks with sandfleas or shrimp.

This fine mangrove snapper blaste[d] [a]
topwater plug in only two feet of wa[ter]

SHARKS

Choice Location: Sharks are the scavengers of both inshore and offshore waters. Just about any body of salt or brackish water will hold some species of shark. Many larger sharks prowling inshore waters are following baitfish schools or some other major food source. The same goes for sharks on the beach, which tend to be most abundant while spawning—or during baitfish runs where they take advantage of plentiful food. In some areas, sharks are common predators in two to four feet of water on inshore flats, and that's where they can really be fun to catch. A 40- to 150-pound shark in shallow water will put on an impressive display of speed, agility and strength, depending on the species.

Choice Baits: Depending on the region, sharks feed on almost everything. In shallow waters of the Gulf and on Southeast Florida flats, best baits are chunks of barracuda, stingray, bonito or jacks. As we move up the Atlantic coast, stingrays, ladyfish, mullet and bunker are good options. In the upper Atlantic, it's bunker, albacore and chunks of bluefish that remain tops. In many cases, it's bloody or oily baits that put a lot of scent in the water, sounding the dinner bell. My personal favorite is a whole ladyfish either alive or dead, but I prefer alive because the strikes can be quite dramatic. SB

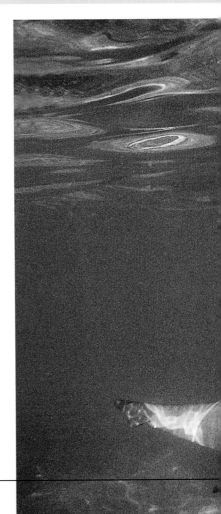

MANGROVE SNAPPER

Choice Location: Just about any inshore structure in South Florida has the potential to hold mangrove snapper. From concrete seawalls to bridge pilings, mangrove roots to boat wrecks, these scrappy little snapper make their homes in structures. They spend their days and nights chasing anything smaller that happens to swim by. The largest fish can be found on nearshore and offshore reefs, and in the inlets during summer and early fall. Given a choice, I prefer to anchor my boat along a nice stretch of mangrove shoreline in four to 10 feet of water, where good clean water exchange takes place.

Choice Baits: Snapper seem to follow the credo that goes, "If it's smaller than me and has eyes, it dies." These little scrappers will eat everything from crabs to chunks of ballyhoo. Glass minnows, silversides and juvenile whitebait are common snapper meals, but a live shrimp floated back to the trees has the words "mangrove meal" written all over it.

Lemon sharks prowl shallow water. This one was hooked on a bonefish jig off Key West.

CHAPTER 7

The Top
Natural Baits

Bait is the great equalizer. It allows an angler to introduce a natural portion of the food chain into the fishing equation. Fish have to be tricked into eating lures, but
bait is the real deal. A fish approaching a live baitfish will
see that baitfish react as it would in the wild. A dead bait
will look, smell and taste like a normal food item.

But there's more to using bait than simply finding it and
pinning it on a hook. You should know what species that
bait will entice. Freshwater fly fishermen call it "matching
the hatch," a term used to explain the concept of figuring
out what fish are eating, and presenting that food to them.
After all, it's going to be a long, unproductive day on the
water if you plan to fish for bluefish or spotted seatrout
with clams.

Knowing the different bait species allows an angler to
understand the options before him on any given fishing
day. It's another part of the puzzle that you try to piece
together every time you go fishing, to figure out what the
fish are feeding on and what to offer. Food is a major motivation for inshore gamefish, and the more you know about
what they like to eat, the better you can match the hatch.

**For better catches, identify your local natural
baits, and know where and how to find them.**

See DVD for more on natural baits.

A school of big mullet, moving like they have a purpose. Biggest baitfish along the Atlantic or Gulf Coasts, mullet convert vegetation into fish protein. Falling prey to bigger gamefish, they feed many species of popular sport fish.

SHRIMP

Common predators: Just about any marine fish that ever swam will eat shrimp, with the exception of some herbivores like mullet. From sheepshead to sand-perch, striped bass to snook, shrimp compose the dietary mainstay of a long list of gamefish. Some fish that really

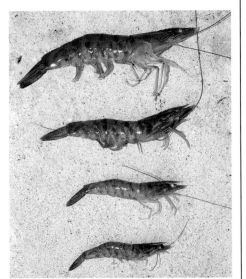

Shrimp are widespread and live in all coastal marshes, where they forage on the bottom.

focus on shrimp are members of the drum family (seatrout, weakfish, red and black drum, whiting and croakers). Snook, tarpon, bonefish, bluefish, pompano,

snapper, jack crevalle, ladyfish and a host of cold water gamefish regularly dine on shrimp during some portion of their life cycles.

How to fish these baits: Although they have a somewhat protective carapace, shrimp are very delicate crustaceans that perish quickly if a hook is placed through any major organs. Avoid hooking the shrimp through the middle of the body or head, if you want it to stay alive for more than a minute. Most anglers hook a shrimp through the horn on the top of the head. Others prefer hooking through the tail, or through the mouth, with the hook coming out of the top of the head.

When fishing for species with small mouths like sand-perch and sheepshead, you can use small pieces of shrimp and thread them onto a hook.

Different shrimp for different folks: Matching shrimp size for your targeted fish is important. Small shrimp attract sheepshead, whiting and pompano, for instance. Jumbo shrimp would be picked out for tarpon and bigger snook. At right, different techniques for hooking shrimp.

Fast action on sheepshead. These anglers are obviously using shrimp or fiddler crabs for bait.

HERRINGS

Common predators: These baitfish are common to Florida waters, and the most important trio consists of the Altantic thread herring, scaled sardine and Spanish sardine. All three are top baits for snook, trout, redfish, tarpon and a host of other gamefish. Normally caught using a cast net or a multiple-hook sabiki bait rig, these baits are fragile and need a well-oxygenated livewell system to remain alive for prolonged lengths of time. They respond well to chumming, which is a common technique for concentrating baitfish on Florida's west coast.

How to fish these baits: They can be hooked several ways, but are most commonly hooked through the nostrils. They can also be hooked in the throat or in the back ahead of the dorsal fin, to make them swim deeper. Placing a hook in the underside just behind the anal fin will make the bait swim toward the surface. Dead baits can be hooked in a similar manner and freelined in the current along with other dead chum baits, which is an effective fishing method for big tarpon.

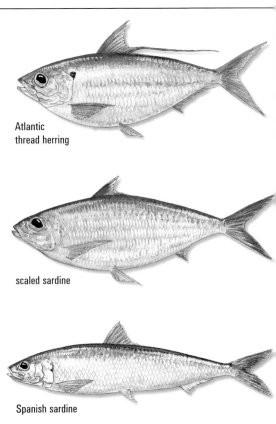

Atlantic thread herring

scaled sardine

Spanish sardine

MULLET

Common predators: Depending on their size, mullet are one of the mainstays of the inshore food chain. As juveniles, they're preyed upon by small gamefish hoping to catch their first live fish meal. Mullet that survive to adulthood are a dietary staple for larger gamefish like sharks, tarpon, barracuda, and mature seatrout, snook and redfish make mullet a staple of their diets. Mullet are herbivores, but can be caught on hook and line using small pieces of dough, but most anglers catch their mullet in a cast net.

How to fish these baits: As live baits, mullet can be hooked through the lips for slow-trolling or to make the bait swim along with the fishing line. When hooked through the throat or dorsal fin a mullet will swim down, which is effective around deepwater bridges and docks. A mullet hooked behind the anal fin will come to the surface, desirable when fishing along the beach or in shallow water. Dead mullet can be cut into strips or chunks and fished on bottom, or they can be used whole for sharks and tarpon. Smaller finger mullet can be fished on bottom for flounder, redfish, bluefish and other scavenging-type gamefish. A mullet head fished on bottom is a top snook and redfish bait.

An able castnetter obviously has an advantage when gathering live bait for the day.

MENHADEN

Common predators: Also known as bunker, shad or pogies, menhaden are baitfish numerous from the Gulf Coast to Maine. Smaller ones used for bait are called peanut bunker, and remain the mainstay for just about every gamefish that forages on finfish. Larger "pogies" are primo baits for trophy striped bass, redfish, tarpon and snook. The oily flesh of of this baitfish them attractive alive or dead to every member of the shark family and many other gamefish. Small pogies are commonly preyed upon by everything from seatrout to bluefish. These guys are so wonderfully fish-attracting, their pure oil is sold in tackle stores as a chum-enhancer.

Fat menhaden pinned to a hook. A great bait for attracting large predators along the beachfront.

How to fish these baits: These baits are extremely fragile and difficult to keep alive even in well-oxygenated systems or bait pens. Small baits can be hooked through the nostrils with a thin wire hook that won't weigh the bait down and hinder natural swimming action. Larger baits can be hooked through the back in front of the dorsal fin, or in the neck or tail. Dead pogies, when cut into chunks and fished on the bottom, are effective for bluefish, red drum and a host of other gamefish.

PINFISH, PIGGY PERCH AND OTHER SMALL FINFISH

Common predators: Every inshore area has its own species of small finfish that can be utilized as bait. Texas has the piggy perch, Florida has the pinfish and sand perch, and the mid- to upper-Atlantic states have their white perch. All these species fall prey to the local list of inshore gamefish. As a rule, larger baits become food to proportionally larger gamefish, while the juveniles are fed upon by gamefish of all sizes.

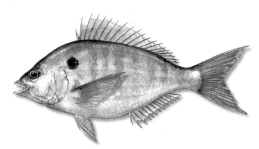

How to fish these baits: Most commonly fished alive, baitfish are hooked through the back in front of the dorsal fin and suspended underneath a cork, especially when fished over shallow grass flats less than five feet down. Over sand or mud bottom, baits are hooked through the cheeks, back or underneath behind the anal fin, and either freelined or fished with the standard slip-sinker rig.

PIGFISH, OTHER GRUNTS

Common predators:
Members of the grunt family are productive baitfish for everything from tarpon to trophy seatrout. Small grunts are commonly utilized in the Florida Keys to catch snapper and grouper, while larger specimens get attacked by barracuda, snook and tarpon. In the Indian River, pigfish are considered the top bait for large spotted seatrout, which are drawn to their constant grunting sounds.

How to fish these baits: Grunts are not strong baits, so they should be hooked and handled gingerly. The majority of anglers fish grunts by hooking them in the back just forward of the dorsal fin and suspending them on a cork rig, so the baitfish remains just above the grass. Around bridges, grunts are allowed to hang four to six feet beneath the cork.

Pigfish rest in a rock jetty puddle before assuming bait duties.

SQUID

Common predators: Squid inhabit inshore and offshore waters, and thus are prey for bigger gamefish. Seatrout, red drum, bluefish, striped bass, flounder and snapper are among their greatest predators when alive. Dead squid will fool whiting, croaker, sandperch and a host of other inshore gamefish. Even sharks will focus on eating squid when the baits are concentrated (or smelly).

How to fish these baits: Live squid aren't a common bait item, although I have caught a fair number of squid in my cast net when after other species. They don't survive in captivity for very long, and are difficult to hook, so they're seldom used as live bait inshore. Dead squid are cut into small strips and threaded onto a hook by placing the point through one end of the strip, then bending it and running the point through the bait several times. A strip of squid can also be used in combination with a jig to add flavor to the offering, and some flounder fanatics prefer a strip of squid along with a live killifish for big "doormat" flounder.

KILLIFISH, COCAHOES, OTHER MUD MINNOWS

Common predators: Mud minnows are one of the most common foods for just about every finfish-eating gamefish. Flounder are probably the most notorious feeders on these

Hardy "mud minnows" (killifish) ready to go to work.

baits, but everything from bluefish and striped bass to snook, trout and redfish find these baitfish delightfully delicious. These tough little baitfish inhabit shallow marshes, drainage ditches and flats with low oxygen, as well as brackish mosquito impoundments and other estuarine environments.

How to fish these baits: Although hearty enough to be kept alive for several days, mud minnows are small baits that require thin wire hooks to prevent major trauma when hooking them. Most commonly hooked through both lips and fished either on a sliding-sinker rig or a jighead, mud minnows work hard on the hook, until something big finds them. This is the easiest saltwater minnow to raise in aquaculture or sell at bait camps, because they're so darn tough.

CRABS

Common predators: There are a host of crab species, and many gamefish feed on crabs at one time or another during their life cycles. Tautog, striped bass, red and black drum, permit, tarpon, sheepshead and bonefish top the list of predators that feed regularly on crabs. Crabs move with the tides, at times latching on to floating grass. They utilize the grass as a means of transport from one area to another. Crab runs typically take place near inlets with the tides, and distinct feeding frenzies sometimes occur. Tarpon, red drum and permit frequently take aim at passing crabs.

Choice fiddler crab ready for a dunking near sheepshead.

How to fish these baits: Crabs can be fished dead or alive, depending on the targeted species. When crabs are moving with the tide, or when you're sight casting to permit and tarpon on the flats and around bridges, a live blue crab is a deadly offering. Hook the crab through the corner of the shell with the hook point entering the underside of the carapace and exiting the top. The bait will remain lively. Large, dead blue crabs can be fished in halves or quarter sections, placed on a hook and cast out on a bottom rig. That's how most of those huge black drum are caught every spring. Live or dead little fiddler crabs are hooked through the body from one corner to the other and fished on a weighted rig, often aimed at sheepshead.

SAND FLEAS

Common predators: Pompano and whiting root in the sand just off the beaches, hoping to find the little mole crab, often called "sand flea" by the surf-fishing public, who fish seriously for pompano. The tiny crabs are easily caught in wet sand at the beach, by dragging one of the rakes pictured below. Some anglers, prepared for a rainy day, keep a few hunded sand fleas frozen at home. They're boiled for only 10 seconds in a mesh bag, before freezing.

How to fish these baits: Commonly pinned to a Kahle-style hook, sand fleas are cast out in the surf with long rods. Most anglers fish with double or triple-hook rigs, so a ready supply of sand fleas certainly helps. Whiting may eat up a number of baits before pompano arrive. Natural beaches without vehicular traffic seem to have more sand fleas than more packed-down beaches.

Above, two models of sand flea rakes used at the beach. At left is the prize; sand fleas (mole crabs) that any pompano would dearly love to find.

Want to catch a big trout? Try rigging a live croaker under a cork or on bottom. These guys can be heard by gamefish a considerable distance underwater.

CROAKERS

Common predators: Just about every species that eats finfish will find croakers an appealing meal. From striped bass to redfish, bluefish, snook and trout, the croaker is a common food source for bigger fish. In Texas, the croaker has proved so effective against large trout, it was hotly debated whether they should even be legal as bait. Since it was impossible to enforce, that idea was dropped by state fishery managers. Lines form at marinas before sunrise, with numerous anglers hoping to "score" a few dozen live croakers, which are mostly caught by bait shrimpboats. The croakers are somewhat battered after being caught, and the most lively and valuable ones are those that have had several days to settle down (or survive) in large circular bait tanks. They're not the liveliest bait, rather weak in fact, but that distress call is their strong suit. They attract gamefish from a distance, even in murky water where visibility is nil.

If you don't want to stand in line or pay for croakers, this is the perfect panfish for kids to catch. They're caught on bottom with bits of shrimp, mostly in summer, and can be stored in a high-volume livewell to target bigger fish later. Many anglers no longer have the time to leisurely catch croakers---they would rather throw down some money for a few dozen and head for their favorite honeyhole.

In Florida, croakers are prized by anglers targeting snook. In the mid-Atlantic states, a live croaker is considered deadly for bluefish, weakfish and striped bass.

How to fish these baits: Smaller baits are typically suspended beneath a cork and hooked either through the back on either side of the dorsal fin. Anglers fishing the surf in Texas with croakers use the standard small egg weight and short mono leader without a cork, hooking them through the upper tail if the current is light. In a stronger current croakers, like any other live bait, must face into the current or they will drown. So they're hooked through the nostrils or both lips. One can set out up to four rods in this manner, waiting for the croaker to sing their siren's song and work their magic.

MARINE WORMS

Common predators: You'd be amazed to know how many inshore species eat worms. The old adage, "even elephants eat peanuts," applies when it comes to worms and striped bass, tarpon and flounder. The palolo worm hatch in the Florida

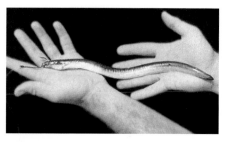

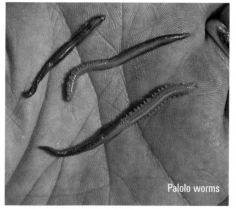

Palolo worms

Keys sends tarpon into a feeding frenzy, and it is the dream of a great many tarpon anglers to be on hand when the water turns orange with these worms in late May or June (no one is ever quite sure when). That's when tarpon and other fish boil the water by the hundreds or thousands, gorging on worms with complete abandon. It is perhaps the easiest way to hook tarpon on fly of anywhere in the world, thanks to the lowly worm.

There are other worms, of course: in the Northeast, some of the largest striped bass each year are caught by anglers fishing the surf with a whole blood worm.

How to fish these baits: Blood worms range in size from two to 18 inches, and can be fished whole for species like stripers, or cut into sections and threaded onto a hook for flounder, porgies and croakers. If the worms are small, several can be placed on a hook at one time to create a large bundle of worms. Palolo worms, even though they grow to a similar size, are not actually used for bait. Fly patterns designed to imitate the worms and copper-colored jerkbaits will fool plenty of these fish when they're feeding in such a frenzy.

EELS

Common predators: Quite a few species feed on eels. Snook and tarpon in particular seem to strike at eels with real aggression. In some areas, sand eels are a favored food of seatrout, cobia, weakfish and fluke. Striped bass and bluefish are probably the top predators of these unique baits.

How to fish these baits: Live eels can be difficult to handle, but most anglers place the eels in a bucket of sand to enable them to get a firm grip on the baits. They can then be hooked through the lips or nose with a single livebait hook. With very large baits, a second tandem hook can be placed in the tail to add a little extra bite for short-strikers. Eels can be cast from shore or boat to a specific fish like a sighted cobia, but for striped bass most anglers simply drift or surf fish with these baits.

CLAMS

Common predators: Red drum, black drum, pompano and striped bass are just a few of the species that can be caught using clams for bait. These species have crushing plates in the back of their throats for mashing mollusks, and are quite adept at finding and consuming them. All four species will take clams from the surf and inshore waters, with specific species of clams being favored over others. In many cases, size and abundance is the most relative factor.

How to fish these baits: For larger fish like trophy stripers and redfish, the clam can be cracked with a hard object or by banging it on concrete. The hook is then inserted into the meat of the clam, and the entire clam is cast out as bait. The most common way to fish clams is to open the clam and remove the meat, place the entire clam on a hook, or cut the clam into strips and then thread them onto the hook. SB

CHAPTER 8

Artificial Lure Strategies

Under most circumstances, it's much harder to fool a fish into eating a lure than some natural bait. So why do anglers subject themselves to the pain of lure fishing? In most cases, it's the challenge of fooling a fish that makes an angler disregard natural bait as an option. Lures allow anglers to not only prospect more water, but also to spend the first hour in the morning fishing, rather than gathering bait. Whatever your reason for using lures, with some practice you'll catch a lot of fish.

If you have a hard time making choices, then you're going to find lure fishing difficult. There are so many options that this is no place for the indecisive. Topwater plugs are visual and produce tremendous strikes, while jigs and soft plastics produce higher numbers of fish. Flies have their own challenge that, when combined with their casting and retrieving limitations, bump the challenge up to an even greater scale.

To be an effective lure fisherman, you really need to understand the action that artificials produce and their best applications. To do that, we need to look at different lure types and their specific traits.

Choosing the best lure for the task at hand. The secret? Carry a variety of different artificials for all occasions.

This mangrove snapper was caught on a topwater plug in Mexico near the border with Belize. Below, a mix of lures ready for action.

Fooling Fish With Artificials

Lure fishermen are thinkers. They really do put a lot of skill and effort into catching fish. To be productive, a lure fisherman often has to be "in the zone," concentrating on his lure, line and surrounding water. While some lures need little or no effort to impart action, others require complete control at all times to make them look natural. That's the water rather softly. For redfish, you want a plug or soft-plastic that hits the water with just a little bit of sound so the fish can locate it.

Lure colors prompt a lot of debate among anglers. Not all color combinations seem natural. High-profile composites like firetiger and electric chicken don't look like anything I've ever seen in the water, but I'm not looking at my food through a fish's eyes. I've never seen a chartreuse mullet, for instance, but under the man-made bridge lights a mullet's back turns chartreuse.

It's hard to go wrong using color patterns that resemble those of the local forage you're

There is an artificial lure for every conceivable fishing scenario. Some dive deep, others wiggle side-to-side or produce an attractive flash.

This bluefish blasted a topwater plug tossed from a surf pier.

real challenge, fooling fish with lures. An angler has to make that plastic or wood come to life.

There is an artificial lure for every conceivable fishing scenario—some that dive deep, some that wiggle side-to-side, some that produce an attractive flash, wiggle or vibration. If you want to make long casts in the surf, you'll find a leadhead jig or weighted plug will cover the distance. When fishing the shallows for bonefish that spook from sound alone, you might pick a tiny skimmer jig that plops in the trying to imitate. A mullet has a black back and silver or white body when inshore, and a blue back and silver or white body when out in the open ocean. Shrimp are white, brown or red. Bunker are yellow with a black spot near the gills. It's okay to experiment with different color schemes, and sometimes you'll find an unusual pattern that just seems to work better than others, for reasons you'll never figure out.

That brings us to specific lure categories. For every action, shape, depth range, sound, and size a lure needs to be, there is a category for it.

Classic shallow-diving plugs and topwaters take a variety of fish. When traveling, always keep a few handy in a small plastic box that fits easily into a wading vest or waders.

Wading angler works a top-water bait over a flat. This requires concentration and timing, and it's easy to miss a tentative strike.

Topwater Lures

Sometimes you'll see the fish open and snap its mouth on the lure.

Of all the lure types, topwater artificials will always find a special place in those fishing memories. Explosive surface strikes take your breath away. A topwater plug entices a fish to the surface while pursuing that bait, where you the angler can see everything. Sometimes you'll even see the fish open and snap its mouth on the lure.

One of my favorite fish to chase with surface plugs is big jack crevalle. A 5- to 10-pound jack will put up a rugged fight on light tackle, but a 30-pounder is a different animal. If you want to step into the house of pain, toss a topwater at a school of jumbo jacks. These schools may be made up of anywhere from 50 to 500 fish, and they roam much of the southeastern U.S. coastal waters. They travel in very tight groups as part of a protective behavior from predators like hammerhead sharks. When a topwater plug lands near the school, a dozen or more fish will chase after it, blasting the lure with such speed and force that they can knock it 10 feet in the air. When one does eat the plug, you're in for a good hour of line-tight action. After catching one (or at most, two) of these big fish, I'll remove the hooks from the lure and cast at the schools, just to watch those ferocious strikes. Few people have the stamina to catch more than a couple of these fish in a day.

But it's not just the aggressive strikes that create the appeal of topwater lure fishing. These lures work, and they work well. They also work on most fish.

The floater/diver is another popular topwater bait. These are usually long and slim baits

with a small lip that makes the lure dive when retrieved with a twitch-pause type of retrieve. When the rodtip is twitched, the lure dives a few inches below the surface, usu-

Hard-hitting jack crevalle like the one above are tough on artificial plugs, including topwater plugs like the chugger-style Knuckle Head, below.

ally making an attractive splash when it dives. At the pause, it floats back to the top. It's during the rise or just as it breaks water that the strikes often take place.

These baits are excellent for fishing over grass beds with sandy potholes, and over rocks or oysters. Because they don't dive very deep, they can be worked in very shallow water. Sometimes it's best to cast to the shallows and work back out to deeper water. Other times it pays to fish from deep back to shallow.

Some good examples of these baits are the Slapstick by Rat-L-Trap, the Rebel and Rapala Minnow series, and the 5M MirrOlure.

Propbaits (with propellers) are great on those calm days when pursuing fish that really use their sense of hearing to locate food. Seatrout and bluefish are notorious for their ability to home-in on the sound of a lure.

Propbaits have little spinners or propellers on one or both ends. As the lure is pulled across the surface, the prop makes an audible sound, as well as creating a splash and bubble trail. The sound draws the predators close, and they sometimes locate the bait by following the bubble trail. Propbaits are an outstanding choice when fishing over grassflats for spotted seatrout, snook and redfish.

Propbaits work much like the floater/divers. They can also be ripped across the surface for several feet at a time and then allowed to rest for a second or two before being ripped again.

These topwaters are famous for their zig-zag action. With a constant, short rod twitch, these guys will perform as they're designed to.

This is good when gamefish are actively chasing baitfish schools in the area. The lone movements of the bait make the gamefish think the lure is just a singled-out bait from a school of fish, no doubt making a dash for freedom. A few examples of propbaits are the 7M Series MirrOLure, the Johnny Rattler and the Heddon Snooker.

Not all of the best topwater lures are big. Some of the best

Nice seatrout and topwater artificial plugs just naturally go hand-in-hand.

Walk-the-Dog

Topwater lures fall into a variety of categories, all of them designed to mimic baitfish. Probably the most common type of topwater lures are walk-the-dog type baits. These are torpedo-shaped lures with two or three treble hooks and swim in a zig-zag pattern, when retrieved with a consistent twitch of the rodtip. Some good examples are the Heddon Zara Spook, MirrOLure Top Dog and Yo-Zuri Walkin' Dog. There are many others like them.

These lures swim with their nose slightly up and tail down, so that a striking fish will grab the rear hooks. The baits come in assorted sizes, and at times it's important to match the size of the lure to the baitfish in your area. If you're seeing mullet six or seven inches long, then you might want a lure of similar size. Going

to a bait that's slightly smaller—say four or five inches— will draw strikes as well, but the larger baits will usually catch the biggest fish.

One of the best applications for walking the dog is fishing around shoreline structure like mangroves, seawalls, docks or bridges. Cast parallel to the structure and swim the lure down it with a side-to-side swagger; many gamefish can't refuse this. You can also cast to the structure at a right angle, in which case you want the lure to land as close to the structure as possible. In many cases the predators will be tight against the structure and not willing to move very far from it. A cast that lands five feet from the mangrove branches might not ever get tangled in the trees, but it won't get hooked up with a snook, either. SB

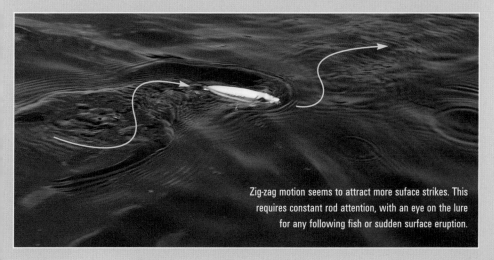

Zig-zag motion seems to attract more suface strikes. This requires constant rod attention, with an eye on the lure for any following fish or sudden surface eruption.

topwaters are under three or four inches in length. When mullet are small, as in late summer and early fall, and beginning to migrate, tiny topwater lures like the Heddon Tiny Torpedo and Yo-Zuri Banana Boat really score. These lures also work fine on small fish like juvenile snook, tarpon and seatrout. Because the lures are small, they have hooks that are proportional to the baits, and these toned-down versions of the larger lures are perfect for catching the youngsters of the gamefish world.

Another common topwater lure is the popper or chugger. These plugs have a flat or concave face that pushes water and air, making a loud pop or chug when the rod tip is twitched hard. To gamefish like a striped bass or redfish, that pop is a feeding call. It tells fish in the immediate area that food is near and it's time to eat.

Poppers can be fished with a steady twitch-pause retrieve, or they can be paused for long

Happy angler at far right with a horseye jack that blasted her topwater plug on the shallow flats. Above is a nice snook that just engulfed a chugger plug. Below are good examples of three chugger/popper lures plus two prop bait lures.

periods. Most anglers prefer to keep the lure moving. Chuggers are really just larger forms of poppers, often with bulging bodies. Chuggers tend to be a lot heavier, usually two to five ounces, designed for surf fishing or slow trolling. They also swim a little deeper in the water, and push a lot more water away from the bait. Fish detect this movement through the lateral lines in their bodies. This moving water also creates the illusion the bait is larger than its size, which will draw

strikes from the largest gamefish.

Poppers work great in shallow water and along skinny water shorelines adjacent to deep water. Also along seawalls, where big fish can pin the bait to the structure when they eat. Chuggers are also outstanding lures in the surf, particularly when worked over a sandbar or across a bar and into a deep trough. Common examples of poppers and chuggers are the Yo-Zuri Hydro Popper, the Pencil Popper and the Arbogast Chugger. SB

Jigs and Bucktails

Jigs are productive because they represent such a wide variety of baitfish. Color combinations are numerous and there are local favorites.

Bonefish nails a small lead-head jig. The lead is kept to a minimum, because these fish are very shy about the lure's splashdown when it arrives.

Jigs have been around for a long time. Original jigs were made of a lead head with a hook in it and either feathers or hair. Those styles remain some of the finest fish-catching lures on the market today. But there's also a lot of new synthetic materials and molded plastic now being utilized for jig production and they also catch their share of gamefish.

Jigs are productive because they represent such a wide variety of baitfish. A white jig looks a lot like a baitfish, while a light brown jig more resembles a shrimp. A yellow and red jig resembles a crab. Pink jigs look like squid.

Color combinations for jigs are numerous and there are local favorites. In Florida a dark green or smoke-colored plastic jig is a trout slayer, while pumpkinseed is often a better color in Texas. The differences are based on local food sources. In Florida, that means Atlantic silversides, while in Texas the jigs may be designed, among other things, to represent even sand eels.

A crab-tipped jig is deadly.

Jig are available in many sizes and shapes. Head design determines sink rate and action. Tails are picked for their underwater action.

Most jigs are worked with an up-and-down retrieve, so the lure rises and falls in the water column. This looks like a crab, shrimp or baitfish.

There is a general rule of thumb when lure fishing, that dark colors work best in dirty water and bright colors do best in bright water. Chartreuse is one of those colors that has applications for both. In clean water, it's a good color for the flats, while in dirty water it's a good color to use at night around bridges. White looks like the side of a baitfish, so it works very well in clear water. Chrome is also good; even pompano will chase after it.

Most jigs are worked with an up-and-down retrieve, so the lure rises and falls in the water column. This action may look like a shrimp or crab diving for the bottom and then rising to the top. Or like a baitfish darting along in an effort to escape. Either way, the majority of strikes come when the lure is falling, so be prepared.

One favorite way to fish jigs is to use a countdown on the retrieve, to place the lure just over the grass. When the lure hits the water, I start counting one-Mississippi, two-

Nice mangrove snapper netted, after it took a small bucktail jig. Below are different sizes and styles, each with its own application.

Mississippi, until I hit a number I think is appropriate for that depth of the water. Let's say the number I count to is six: At the right count, retrieve the lure in a normal manner. If the lure catches grass on the retrieve, count to five and follow the same retrieval pattern. When the lure can be retrieved without catching grass, it's swimming just above the grass—where fish can lunge after it.

The different hair-type materials used for jigs and how they are tied to the lead head are determined by the application. If you want a jig to show a large profile, the lure has to be tied with a large amount of hair. Or the hair has to be tied onto the leadhead in reverse, so that it flares around the head and makes the jig look twice as big as it actually is.

A lot of anglers prefer their jigs more streamlined, so the lure can be tied with less hair than normal to make it slide through the water column more efficiently. Tied this way, a jig will sink quicker using less lead. For fish that have small mouths or are notorious short strikers like pompano, the hair of the jig can be cut right at the back of the hook so that if the fish grabs it from the rear, it will surely get a surprise.

The size of the lead will usually be proportional to the rest of the jig, so the size of the jig will determine casting range and sink rate of the lure. For most shallow water fishing a 1/8- or 1/4-ounce jig is the lure of choice, while bridge fishermen or anglers after large fish might want a 1- or 2-ounce jig. The heavier the jig the faster it sinks, so even though heavy jigs cast better, they're more likely to get your lure tangled in grass or

Bounce Your Bucktail

One of the most popular jigs in Florida is the Red Tail Hawk jig, which is a lure designed to catch snook. These jigs have a white or red lead head, and a chartreuse or white body with a long strip of red hair that extends an inch or so past the end of the other hair.

The Red Tail jig, wtih its distinctive trailing tail, is the most popular of all snook jigs.

This trailer section of red hair looks like a tail under water and gives the jig some natural swimming motion. The Red Tail Hawk is one of the few jigs retrieved with little or no action.

I can't tell you how many snook I've caught in Florida with this jig, but it numbers in the thousands. And many of those fish were big. My standard trick for fishing the jig at night from bridges was to carry a flashlight and a handful of jigs in white or chartreuse. I would walk out on the bridge and shine the flashlight into the water. If the water was clean and clear I would use the white jig. If it was milky or dirty I would use chartreuse. SB

structure unless you're fishing deep water.

The shape of the lead head can determine the action of the lure. A jig with a thin, flat head might be the best option on the flats, with a wobble that appeals to bonefish. Rounded jig heads aren't as likely to catch on bottom structure like oysters and rocks, and jig heads

with a lip dive faster than another shape of similar weight.

Probably the most common jigs on the market today are the standard bucktails made of deer hair tied to a lead head. In most cases the lead head is painted and often a different color than the bucktail. Bucktail jigs are very effective for most inshore gamefish, and can be colored to look like everything from baitfish to small shrimp.

The old-style chicken feather jigs aren't around as much, but they're still very consistent fish catchers. Some of the new, synthetic hairs have a gloss or shine that fish can't resist. They also have stiffness properties that

Bonefish at top grabbed a tiny jig on the flats. These speedsters prefer small crustaceans as bait, and the jig certainly fills that niche. The color and tail material used in making jigs is often brightly colored, for subdued lighting found underwater.

give the lure more undulation.

Jigs are a very consistent lure choice for fish of all species and sizes and something that should be in every angler's tackle box. If I were a betting man, I'd say more fish have been caught on jigs than all the other lure options combined. SB

Skimmer Jigs

Skimmer jigs, also called bonefish jigs or flathead jigs, are designed for shallow water. A skimmer jig's head is flattened horizontally, rather odd-looking compared with standard jigs. They tend to ride and lay on bottom with the hook up. When you tick it across mud or sand bottom it sends up puffs of sediment to catch a predator's attention. It's a real turn-on for fish, and can readily pass for a crab, shrimp or small baitfish. Skimmer jigs have possibly taken the greatest variety of shallow-water fish on a steady basis, because you can always add the finicky bonefish to that list, a fish that won't grab just any jig. Skimmers are available in a variety of colors, typically weigh from 1/8 to 1/4 ounce in size, and should have weed-guards for fishing the grassflats. SB

Pompano love crustaceans more than anything else. This one grabbed a brightly colored skimmer jig that must have looked like a crab.

Corks and Floats

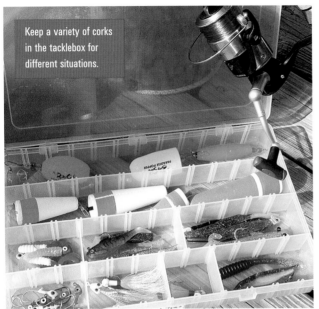

Keep a variety of corks in the tacklebox for different situations.

Any gamefish nearby that hears the cork seems to think another fish is feeding nearby.

There is something to be said for the principles of suspension. The ability to place a lure or bait above structure or grass gives anglers a big advantage, holding that bait in the strike zone for longer periods of time. That really helps the fish see the bait.

Corks and floats are available in a lot of different shapes and styles, with different purposes. The most common saltwater corks are made of Styrofoam or natural cork.

Styrofoam corks come in a variety of shapes, but the most popular over the years has been the popping cork. It's tubular with a concave top that chugs and pops when the angler yanks on the line. This "popping" sounds just like a fish when it strikes at the surface. Any gamefish nearby that hears the cork seems to think another fish is feeding nearby. As that fish moves toward the sound, it eventually finds the bait suspended

under the cork and grabs an easy meal.

Popping corks are available in several styles, with and without weights. The most common have a small lead weight built into the cork—a distinct advantage when casting. The extra weight helps deliver the small bait underneath.

These weighted corks also benefit casters on windy days. When casting into the wind, the cork can be thrown in a flat arc, to limit wind resistance on the cork and bait. When casting with the wind, the cork is cast in a higher arc, which allows the wind to really carry it.

Some popping corks are built with a wire or mono leader and sliding sinker attached. This rig allows the angler to use a bobber stop above the weight to limit the depth the sinker will take the bait. Since the sinker is below the cork, it will pull the bait down to a specific depth until the bobber stop locks into place and suspends the bait below the cork at the desired depth. This type of rig is most commonly used in deepwater applications where the water is over six feet in depth, like jetty fishing.

Unweighted corks are used when fishing with baits that are fairly large, or when long casts aren't necessary. Some anglers prefer popping corks because of the extra noise, while others prefer to use quiet, round natural corks for their better flotation qualities. Both have their merits, but popping corks carry the advantage with their dual ease of use and sound advantage.

Besides longer casting and sound, the main advantage to using corks is their ability to hold or suspend a bait at a desired depth. Watch the depthfinder, and rig the cork and bait accordingly, to avoid snagging grass, oyster or bottom. Holding the bait just above structure puts it right in front of the fish. Remember, fish have eyes that look upward, so they're more likely to see a bait suspended above them than right on bottom.

When fishing live bait with corks, there are several places to hook a bait to get a desired action. For instance, hooking a croaker or pinfish near the tail on the dorsal side allows the bait to pull and wiggle in a more constant fashion. Hook it near the head, and it yanks the baitfish around, any time it pulls the leader tight. That tends to stress out the bait. In a constant current, hook them through the lips or nostrils, so they face into the current. You certainly don't want them spinning in the current. Shrimp under corks can be hooked just under their sharp horn, or near the tip of the tail.

Corks are a good way to keep track of your lines, so they don't cross and tangle. Redfish, left, grabbed a jig dangling under the cork.

The rattle cork originated from Port Mansfield, on the Laguna Madre. An entire genre of these corks has spread across the Gulf Coast.

Rattle cork at rest. Beads and swivels impact when the line is yanked, below, creating sound.

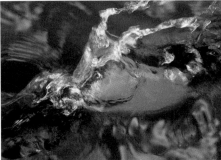

With a twitch of the rod tip, modern "rattle corks" are rigged to click and snap while sliding up and down on a wire. The click imitates the sound of a shrimp trying to escape. They've also become far more popular than older (but still Styrofoam) "pop corks." Rattle corks are neon green and orange and colored to stay visible even in whitecaps or tall grass.

Way down in Port Mansfield on the South Texas coast, Capt. Bob Fuston is widely credited with building the first rattle cork, called the Mansfield Mauler. Others since have changed the design slightly, or the shape, making them more bulbous or adding weights and various, colorful beads.

Bob's original cork and others that soon followed were three inches long and the width of a finger, fairly easy to cast against the wind. The cork slid up and down an eight-inch wire, clicking loudly when beads hit swivels. Trout and redfish like it so much they often attack the cork, sometimes biting them in half. A 2- or 3-foot mono leader is

Angler grabs the heavier leader below his rattle cork, to land redfish.

attached to the bottom swivel, with a hook at the end, or even a plastic shrimp or leadhead grub, which makes the cork even more popular.

Original Mansfield Mauler cork with live baitfish attached.

What's interesting about the rattle cork is that it's been very popular in Texas for so long, but has been slow to catch on in other areas. The first Florida company tried to introduce the product, but after years of beating their corks against the wall, gave up. But it seems the clickety-clackety cork is finding a home in growing numbers. It just takes seeing it work more than once to convert even the oldest dog in the pack.

Rattle corks are now sold pre-rigged or alone. Some models are wider and louder on the water, perhaps even with a cupped mouth for extra noise (in murky water). As for leaders below the cork, anglers in clear water prefer to use modern fluorocarbon instead of mono. The leader can be lightened as the water becomes even more clear.

Fishing guides like the rattle corks because an angler without much experience, or even a boatload of it, can catch a variety of fish, even while using soft artificial baits underneath. All they have to do is get the cork out there and keep popping it. When it disappears, set the hook or at least reel fast. Often the worst fisherman in the boat catches the biggest trout of the day, using these corks. They're commonly used in places like the coastal bend of Florida on the Gulf Coast, where healthy seagrass covers the bottom for many miles. Drifting in five feet of water, with a leader three feet long, this cork and jig combo refuses to hang up on bottom, and catches fish all day. The leadheaded grub worm or plastic shrimp underneath dances and flits around, and those with a twister tail really put on a show.

On those same drifts, someone who is tired of casting can rig up a live pinfish and drag it along with the boat, back upwind. Bingo! Another big trout of the day. Though there are far too many hungry pinfish in the grass to use live shrimp under these corks, local anglers have devised the perfect anti-pinfish natural bait. They use the upper or lower half of a headless pinfish, cut right along the backbone, with half of the tail fin attached to the two baits. It's called "shiner fishing." The offering looks like the choice part of a pinfish, left behind after some vicious attack, but it dances around in a streamlined shape like a finger mullet. Pinfish have an aversion to cannabalism, at least when they can recognize the bait, and avoid it like the plague. They just have a thing about eating Cousin Freddy or Uncle Ned. Gamefish don't suffer these same qualms; it's fairly common for anglers to return to the marina with trout and Spanish mackerel up to 5 pounds, after using the rattle cork and pinfish combo. SB

Newer model rattle cork with old-fashioned, concave mouth, to create maximum splash and noise.

Swimming Plugs

Every tackle box should have a good selection of swimming plugs. Swimming plugs have inshore and nearshore applications, from fishing deep water around bridges for stripers to trolling for kingfish on the beach.

I rarely used swimming plugs until I went fishing for cobia in Charleston, South Carolina. A friend and I were seeing a fair number of fish, but they were turning their noses up at our jigs. My friend grabbed a lighter rod that happened to have a swimming plug on it from his last bass fishing trip, and on the first cast a fish raced to eat the

plug. After landing the fish, we caught up to the pod of cobia and once again they only wanted a swimming plug. We landed six cobia that day and every one of them was on that plug. We had to take turns with the lure, and every hooked fish brought lots of advice from others on how to not lose our only working plug.

Most swimming plugs are built so they float on or near the surface and many have plastic or metal lips. The idea behind a swimming plug is that it represents a baitfish at rest on the surface, that decides to move. The action you give a plug will determine

The idea behind a swimming plug is that it represents a baitfish at rest on the surface, that suddenly decides to move.

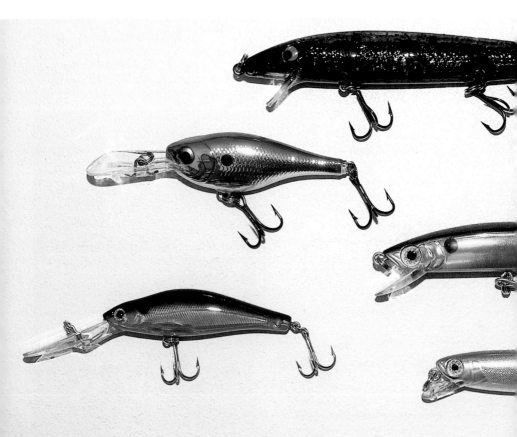

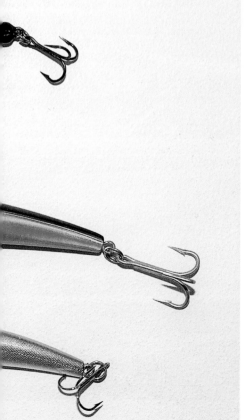

Diving plugs work well, if you have enough water depth. The barracuda above couldn't resist this diver. Below, a trophy bluefish attacked this shallow-diving plug and certainly made someone's day.

how its movements are interpreted.

If you want the lure to give the impression of a panicked baitfish, then rip it along with long strokes of the rod, followed by short pauses. This will make the lure dive and swim forward four to six feet. As the lure is paused, it floats back to the surface. While it rises to the top, the fish will attack. I've caught a lot of big seatrout in Louisiana and Texas using this technique.

These types of lures can also be retrieved with a slow, steady swimming action, where the lure moves along with a side-to-side swagger. In this case, the lure isn't paused at all. Predators see this as an unsuspecting baitfish swimming along, and attack the lure while still in motion. This is good technique for fishing a lure along the beach, where it swims parallel to shore like a migrating baitfish. It's also good for night fishing along a bridge or dock pilings.

Predators see this as an unsuspecting baitfish swimming along, and attack the lure during its constant motion.

Probably the best application for this type of retrieve is to reel it above structure that almost reaches the surface. Reefs, rocks and oyster bars that have holes and crevices have lurking gamefish that often attack any baits that swim overhead. This is very common during baitfish runs, when predators know what's on the menu. Tide and current are key factors with this type of fishing. The fall mullet run also stacks a variety of species along beachfront rock jetties, where a swimming plug worked slowly along can be deadly.

The size of the lip on a swimming plug determines how deep it dives. Some lipped plugs are meant to swim down only a few feet. The lips on these lures are wide and short. The width gives the lure a lot of swagger, and the length determines the depth at a set retrieve rate. A lot of striped bass and redfish lures used in the surf have these traits. The lures are eight to 12 inches long and weigh several ounces, so they can be cast over breaking waves and out to an offshore bar. As the lure is retrieved, it swims a few feet below the surface, where a big striper can charge up and crush the bait as it comes over the bar. SB

Trolling Lures

One of the most effective applications for swimming plugs is trolling, which is something of a lost art. It works both inshore or along the beaches, where it's fun and effective for a large variety of fish. As a general rule, when trolling, select a lure and trolling speed that allows you to get to the strike zone without hanging bottom. Obviously the faster you go, the deeper a big-lip plug will dive, but at some point the lure is moving too fast for fish to catch it. Most anglers prefer to troll at 2 to 4 knots on inshore waters.

Plugs with small lips will swim anywhere from three to 10 feet down. If you're trolling for grouper or trout along a channel edge in 10 feet of water, you can slow your speed and get the lure to swim seven or eight feet down, putting it right above bottom and directly in front of fish. When seeking big redfish in the inlets, the water will be deeper, so a swimming plug with a big lip works better. For chasing stripers and jumbo blues off the beach, the big lips that dive 20 feet or more are the best. SB

Sinking/Diving Plugs These plugs have a

Probably the most overlooked lure category is the sinking/diving plugs, particularly the deep divers. If fish are sitting in a deep hole, or you're fishing off some tall structure like a bridge or seawall, a sinking plug can be a good choice because it allows your lure to get below the surface and right in front of the fish.

Most sinking/diving plugs are lures with a neutral buoyancy or are weighted for a slow to medium sink rate. Some are fast sinkers.

Sinking/diving plugs are great for those cooler months when fish aren't responsive to topwater plugs. They're also good for fishing structure. And don't overlook the use of these lures during the heat of the day, when fish have moved off the flats and into deeper water.

I've always been a fan of the 52M11 MirrOlure for winter trout fishing. When the water temperature drops and the fish move to channels and edges of flats, that's when this medium-sinking plug really works. The lure has a red head and white body (called Woody Woodpecker in Texas), which gives it a lot of contrast in dirty water. And because it sinks three to five feet, it can be worked over submerged structure and deeper grass that hold these cold-water fish. I like to give the lure

some action on the retrieve, with a couple of twitches of the rodtip, followed by a short pause. The strikes happen during the pause. It's an outstanding winter lure for just about any region, but has really found a home for winter trout in Florida waters.

Most sinking/diving plugs have a side-to-

A variety of sinking, shallow-diving plugs. These lures all catch plenty of fish, and should find a place in that tacklebox for the salty angler.

side action in the water, when you retrieve them. For instance, with a neutral buoyancy plug, reel and make two or three twitches of the rod tip, then pause, and follow with two more twitches, repeating until the lure is back to the boat.

The twitching of the rod will make the lure dart from side-to-side, and the pause will allow it to remain motionless for a second or two like a disoriented baitfish.

Size and shape also determine swimming action. Lures have built-in lips you can "tune" with pliers to make the lure favor one direction. A great technique when you have solid

Dinner on the table! Schooling Spanish mackerel will readily attack flashy baitfish imitators like the MirrOlure above and Rat-L-Trap below.

structure you want the lure to bang against or swim away from. Snook and striped bass regularly pin mullet and other baits against sailboat keels and other structure. If you make the lure swim alongside it you might get a strike, but a lure bouncing off the keel looks like a frantic bait. Guess which gets more attention?

I really prefer lipped plugs for fishing parallel to seawalls. Trout, snook, tarpon and jacks will jump on one of these plugs as it swaggers down the wall, with limited direction of escape. Often these fish blast the lure with

such force that the fish clears the water. Barracuda are famous for this type of reverse aerial attack. And if you really want to see them go wild, break the lip off one of the plugs so that the wobble is tripled. Retrieve it twice as fast as normal; even a barracuda has to scramble to catch up with the lure. When it does, it happens with authority.

Most of these swimming plugs are made of hard plastic, but there are also some soft-plastic models on the market. The Corky is built in floating and sinking models, with a cork insert designed to control buoyancy. This lure was designed to imitate mullet and is worked with a side-to-side twitching pattern, like most others of that nature. The soft-plastic body fools a fish into thinking it has grabbed something real.

I don't see a lot of anglers using deep-sinking plugs like I used to. Years ago, the mullet-shaped deep sinkers were the main staples for tarpon fishing in southeast Florida and off the

Lipless Divers

Lipless crankbaits that don't float fit into the category of sinking lures with a side-to-side swimming action. Some of the most common are the Rat-L-Trap, Berkley Frenzy and Cordell Swimming Spot. These lures are weighted for longer casts and will sink right to the bottom if you let them. A slow retrieve keeps them wiggling deep, a nice feature in a lure. It allows an angler to count down several seconds before starting the retrieve. If the lure bumps bottom, the countdown should be shorter on the next cast. If it's not getting deep enough, the count-

These sinking divers, such as the Rat-L-Trap, are good for casting or slow trolling.

down can be longer. Find the right count, and it's almost easy. I've seen guys catch a dozen snook in a row with this technique, when they hit the right count and then retrieved slowly.

Lipless crankbaits are outstanding for fishing around inlets, seawalls and areas of deep water with lots of current. Their shape best mimics fish in the shad, herring and bunker families, favorite baits for just about every major inshore gamefish. SB

Keys bridges. These lures had two hooks and weighed about an ounce, and they got down into the water column quickly. Off tall bridges they allowed anglers to reach the fish suspended deep or just off bottom. When the fishing was really good, it was common to have a tarpon eat the lure and then throw it on the first or second jump, and then have that lure get attacked again as it was reeled back in. Two strikes on one cast—that's a good sign on any day. SB

The Rat-L-Trap is extremely popular in many regions. This angler wore out dozens of snook while casting and trolling these plugs during his visit to Honduras.

This South Texas redfish couldn't resist a red worm shaped so it will undulate through the water.

Soft Plastics

In the last two dozens years or so, soft-plastic baits have really gained notoriety. The first plastic baits on the market were just glorified worms from the bass industry. These lures had long, tubular shapes with a shrimp or fish-shaped tail, and they worked.

New chemical combinations allowed for softer plastic materials and a rapid expansion in lure types in the saltwater market. Injection molding became a construction technique that any promising lure inventor could master with a handful

Anglers have quickly learned that because these baits are soft, fish hold on to them longer. That certainly helps in catching them.

of soft plastic, a beaker and a microwave. All it required was a mold to pour it in.

Besides being easy to work with, pliable plastics gave lures more swimming action. Anglers quickly learned, too, that because it was soft, fish held onto it longer, allowing those anglers "asleep at the reel" to still have a chance at a hookset. With the advent of softer plastics came major changes in shapes and sizes, as different lure manufacturers experimented with new plastic materials.

Soft-bodied jigs are available today in huge numbers. Compared to natural hair-type jigs, the soft plastics have more flex while retaining their natural size. This gives the lure more action while still looking authentic.

Plastic shrimp were the next addition to the soft-plastic realm. The advantages over natural shrimp are obvious: plastics are durable and don't require a bait bucket or aerator to keep alive.

Soft-plastic shrimp like the D.O.A. series are outstanding for a large variety of gamefish. They look, swim, jump and act like natural baits. These lures can be rigged weedless by adding a small piece of wire or plastic ahead of the hook, and they can also be rigged on a leadhead to make the lure swim deep.

See DVD for more on plastics.

Other soft-plastic baits include tube lures, eels and plastic crabs. Small tube lures look like anything from squid to crab, while larger surgical tube lures are made to resemble needlefish darting through the water, something that drives most barracuda, above, crazy. Plastic eels are made to resemble sand eels; some are weighted to get them deep off the beaches where larger striped bass and bluefish roam. Baitfish and shrimp jigs are colorful, numerous and each has its own degree of wiggle and flash. SB

The simple plastic shrimp above swims upright and is certainly tough to beat when fooling fish. Below are more shrimp imitations, along with various and colorful baitfish jigs.

Jerkbaits

Jerkbaits are a more recent addition to the world of soft plastics. These are available in a variety of sizes, shapes and colors, but it's the arbitrary swimming action of this lure that makes it so attractive to hungry gamefish. A small jerkbait with a dark color can be made to look like an escap-ing shrimp, by giving the rod regular twitches and then letting the lure fall. It can mimic a dying mullet by planing to the top and letting it flutter back down. The erratic action of these lures allows an angler to fish the same lure like several different forage species, and that's a distinct advantage over other lures.

Some jerkbaits have shrimp-like tails and rigid bodies to make the lure snap more in the water like a jumping shrimp. Others have fish-like tails or funky designs with a fat body and streamlined tails that vibrate through the water on the retrieve much like a fish's tail.

The key to effectively fishing jerkbaits is rigging them correctly. Most are designed to be rigged Texas-style, with off-set bass worm hooks. Hook companies manufacture products for the saltwater market that rust a lot slower than freshwater bass hooks. Rigged this way, the point of the hook remains buried inside the bait, rendering the lure weedless. That's a major advantage in certain situations. When?

There are times of the year when seagrasses die off and float to the surface. On these days fishing plugs with multiple treble hooks is an exercise in frustration—but a jerkbait is right at home. The same goes for low tide periods when the grass beds, oyster bars, mangroves and other marine structure limit the ability to fish normal hooked plugs. You can swim jerkbaits right through, over and above these structures, and then drop it into a hole to draw an aggressive strike.

There are also times when you want to get a little deeper

Jerkbaits are deadly on stripers, above. Below are steps for Texas-rigging, to make a jerkbait weedless. Notice the worm-style hook.

with your jerkbait or make a longer cast. That's the time to add some weight. There are weighted hooks that still allow the lures to be rigged Texas-style. In most cases, the weight rides along on the upper end of the hook shank close to the eye. On at least one hook style, the eye has an additional pin-like appendage that goes into the top of the jerkbait, to anchor the hook into the bait. Some anglers forgo the special weighted hooks and add a leadhead to the lure.

Leadheads have several functions, but the primary job is to add weight to the lure. Many leadheads are colored and also have eyes painted onto them. Colors add contrast to the lure, so fish can see it better in dirty water, and those eyes give predators a sense of which direction the target will likely move.

When fishing jerkbaits, I prefer to go with the lightest leadhead I can get away with. In most cases, that means a 1/8-ounce head. This little bit of lead will get a bait down under the surface or down to the bottom in the shallows where it can work its magic over the grass. If you're looking to bump the bottom, a 1/4-ounce leadhead is a better option.

I really like the 1/8-ounce leadhead when fishing jerkbaits over grass or along shallow

shorelines, and prefer 1/4-ounce leadheads when fishing over sand. The heavier leadhead will allow the bait to bounce off the sand, creating little puffs that gamefish take for an escaping meal.

Below, various plastic worm tails threaded on to jigheads. Above, circle hooks threaded straight onto jerkbait tails and one with a weighted hook.

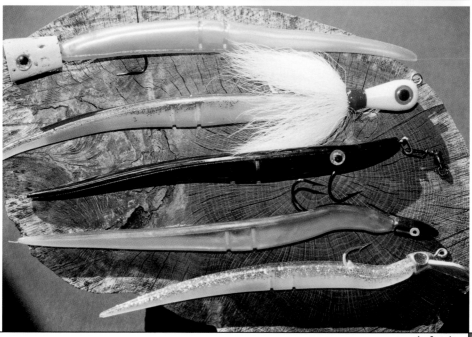

Spoons

The spoon is a universal lure for inshore and nearshore fishing across the country. These metal lures with a single or treble hook produce a swimming action with a flash that gamefish can't resist. Best of all, they're easy to work on the water; most only require a steady retrieve.

Spoons often are used to target specific species like redfish, bluefish, striped bass, trout and Spanish mackerel. The shape of the spoon determines its action, as well as what depth it will swim. Weight is another factor of depth, but some spoons such as the Nemire Red Ripper, Tony Acetta Gold Spoon and Johnson Silver Minnow, are designed to swim at or just below the surface, so they can be worked in

This style of gold spoon has long been the favorite of wading surf fishermen, seeking trout and redfish on the Texas coast.

shallow water over grass and other bottom. Some are rigged with a weedguard to keep from catching grass.

Most spoons have a wide body and are slightly bent or concave. They're designed to be cast a good distance, and in shallow water the retrieve can be started as soon as the lure hits the water—so they don't bog down in the grass. The retrieval speed controls the depth, with a faster retrieve popping it to the surface. The spoon's shape also imitates certain bait species. A spoon with a wide body at the top tapering down at the bottom (where the hook is) will have a lot of wobble and flash like a big bunker or shad.

Another spoon with less flare at the top will swim with a more streamlined wobble, much like a sardine, mullet or other small bait-fish. Thin spoons with minimal tapering are designed to be more aerodynamic, so they fly through the wind with less resistance. A good example is the Hopkins spoon series, designed for long casts off the beach or from break-waters. These lures look like the thick end of a flattened butter knife, but they cast farther than most spoons on the market. The lack of resistance in this shape also makes them move faster through the water, a factor in fooling fast-moving gamefish like Spanish mackerel.

The weight of a spoon will often determine the casting distance and how fast the lure sinks. In most inshore estuaries, a 1/8- to 3/8-ounce spoon is the norm, and to southern wade-fishing pros, any-thing over that weight bracket is considered excessive. Heavier

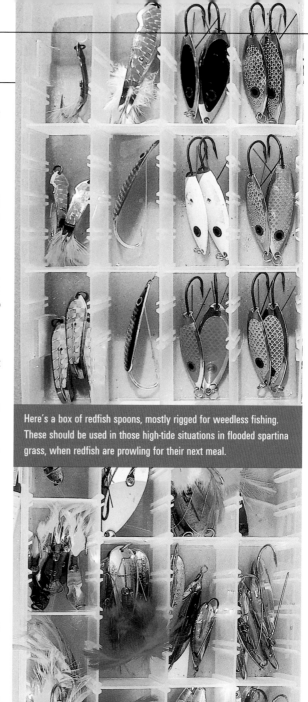

Here's a box of redfish spoons, mostly rigged for weedless fishing. These should be used in those high-tide situations in flooded spartina grass, when redfish are prowling for their next meal.

spoons have applications for anglers who want to get their lures down deep or reach out to fish with that extra-long cast. Spoons in weights of one to three ounces are fairly common, but when stripers or big reds are a long cast from shore, a 4- or 5-ounce spoon may be required.

Some spoons are very small, designed to resemble small, juvenile baitfish. When trolling for Spanish mackerel along the beach, a small but flashy spoon is preferred because of the mackerel's small mouth and slashing strikes. These fish are usually targeting small minnows, and the larger spoons not only don't

Another travel kit filled with spoons and plastic trailers. Keep a variety handy for almost any situation.

resemble what's on the menu, but they also miss a lot of striking fish. Spoons come with single and treble hooks. Single hooks are far easier to remove from a fish, of course.

Common spoon colors include silver or gold, though they are made in just about every color of the rainbow. Some are multi-colored.

Spoon Tails

A fair number of spoons on the market arrive with some sort of trailer or plastic skirt, perhaps a small red dot or soft-body grub with a swimming tail. These trailers add more action and coloration to a lure, to make them appear more lifelike. The most common example is a pink or chartreuse swimming tail, added to the single hook of a gold spoon to entice redfish. Trailers can be effective additions to your spoons, but make sure you carry backups for when the fish tear those trailers off during a hard fight—and you're suddenly stuck with a spoon with limited swimming action.

You can also add a trailer of your own. There are several companies that make plastic skirts, swimming-tail grubs and even shaped pork rinds for trailers. Be sure to make the trailer smaller than the spoon, or it will inhibit the casting distance and swimming action. Along the beach, a section of plastic surgical tubing can be placed over a single hook on a spoon to give the lure more color and an eel-like profile. SB

Because spoons swim with a constant action and resemble a number of baitfish species, they're commonly used for inshore and nearshore trolling. It doesn't take much preparation to tie on a couple of spoons, put the boat in gear, and let them back a specific distance. In this case, the boat does the searching, and the spoon fools the fish.

Boat speed is usually faster than most anglers can reel, so an extra weight or planer can be added to the line to get the spoon down deeper. During summer when certain fish (striped bass or king mackerel) lie deep in the water column but inside the inlets, a spoon with a cigar weight in front of it can be made to swim just over the bottom, passing right in front of big fish. Most planers swim at a very specific depth range marked on their package, and you can select the right planer for a spoon by knowing the local water depth or closely

This redfish took a lighweight Hakala Willow Spoon, a weedless spoon for grass bottom.

monitoring the depthfinder on the boat.

It should be mentioned that the natural action of some spoons—but not all —is to spin. Constant spinning can really put a twist in your fishing line and render it unusable. To avoid line twist, always add a swivel to your line above the spoon, preferably where the leader joins the line. The faster the retrieve, the better quality the swivel should be, and ball bearing swivels should be considered while trolling. SB

There's something inherently fun about catching fish on a fly, just a carefully crafted assemblage of feathers, fur and nowadays, synthetic materials of all kinds. Unlike molded plastic, flies have to be tied and shaped with care. There's as much skill in creating the fly as in fishing it.

Flies are as versatile as the human imagina-

tion. Much of a fly's allure for tarpon and bonefish, for instance, is action with little overall movement. Unweighted flies can be suspended and allowed to remain motionless for long periods right in front of a fish. They can also be hopped off the bottom and allowed to rest, appearing to be prey hiding on bottom. These two species, along with redfish,

See DVD for more on inshore flies.

Fly gear is extensive and intimidating to the neophyte, but rewards are great when it all comes together.

For every gamefish species there are as many (or more) fly patterns as there are lures, so where to start? Generally, you want to match the fly to local forage available, but don't be afraid to tie on something totally unlike the common forage, if fish don't take your initial choice. If the fish are eating minnows, then try a minnow pattern. If they want shrimp or crabs, then fish those fly patterns primarily. If they're eating mullet off the surface, perhaps a popper or slider pattern will work best.

Some of the most commonly used inshore patterns are small, unweighted flies designed to look like finfish, two to four inches in length.

A large percentage of finfish species have white coloration in their body, most often on the side, so an all-white fly can resemble everything from a pilchard to a mullet.

The main advantages to unweighted fly patterns are that they're easy to throw and have a

are highly sought after by fly fishermen because they allow for sight casting to approaching fish. More often than not the angler gets to see the fish locate the fly, track and eat it. Watching a 100-pound tarpon swim up behind a shrimp pattern, open and literally suck in a gallon of water (along with your fly) is quite a sight.

slow or neutral sink rate. Those are major advantages when chasing inshore gamefish. The slow or negative sink rate allows a fly to remain in the strike zone for long periods, and lets you work the fly over the top of most structure, like grass bottom. If the fly only sinks a few inches below the surface, it is riding above the fish, and that's good. Remember that some fish have eyes that face upward, so they're more likely to see this type of fly in shallower water. Good examples include

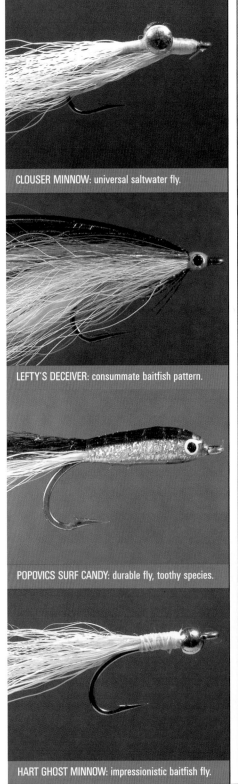

CLOUSER MINNOW: universal saltwater fly.

LEFTY'S DECEIVER: consummate baitfish pattern.

POPOVICS SURF CANDY: durable fly, toothy species.

HART GHOST MINNOW: impressionistic baitfish fly.

snook, tarpon, stripers and seatrout.

Weighted flies have a purpose, and that is to sink quickly to a specific strike zone. Depending on the amount of weight, these flies can be no problem to cast, or quite difficult. The amount of weight and overall bulk of the fly determines the sink rate. The most common patterns sink at a rate of one to four inches or so per second. These are made to order for "down-feeders" such as bonefish, red and black drum and permit. Weighted flies are

Of all the many fly patterns, I have

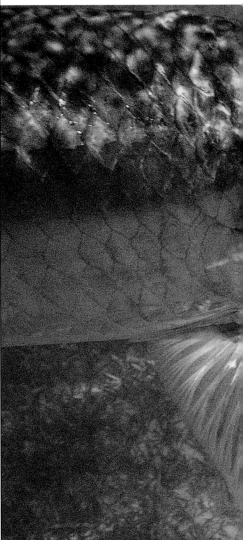

in constant motion, although there are some applications where you might pause for short periods over sand or mud bottom. In most cases, the fly is designed to get to a specific depth and stay there—usually for the entire retrieve, often without the use of a sinking fly line. These types of flies can resemble small bucktail jigs in shape, sink rate and effectiveness at mimicking a variety of marine species. A pink or brown weighted fly will likely resemble a shrimp, while a white or chartreuse weighted fly looks more like a baitfish. Weighted flies are very effective for most inshore species, particularly around water over four feet in depth.

Of all the many fly patterns, I have a special place in my tacklebox for flies that stay on top. Poppers, sliders and other surface-running patterns draw those explosive surface strikes that we all live for. Unfortunately, they're for special times when fish are not shy about feeding on the surface. A school of gamefish milling

cial place in my tacklebox for flies that stay on top.

Big tarpon eat very small flies, by comparison. This hundred-pounder was in eight feet of water off Key West.

on the surface is a prime chance to fish these patterns. When fish are in a feeding frenzy on top, popper and slider flies really come into their own.

Because poppers create a sound like a feeding fish, you can sometimes draw fish such as seatrout, bluefish and snook to them from

Sea-Ducer suspending fly for shallow water fishing took this fine Texas seatrout.

quite a distance.

Shrimp flies can be weighted or unweighted, even made of molded synthetic materials to resemble the real item. Most are weighted so they rise and fall through the water column, much like a real shrimp. These flies are bounced along with aggressive strips of the line, giving the impression the shrimp has spotted the predator and is kicking its tail to escape. Because so many inshore salt waters hold shrimp, a shrimp fly will take most inshore gamefish.

It would be remiss to not include a few universal fly patterns. The Lefty's Deceiver is tied in various sizes to mimic a wide variety of baitfish. I'm a big fan of the new synthetic hair materials and favor a pattern called the Polar Fibre Minnow for everything from striped bass to tarpon.

The Clouser Deep Minnow has lead eyes and swims through the water column much like a jig, yet it can be tied to resemble every-

thing from shrimp and crabs to large baitfish. Pick a coastal state, and the inshore gamefish there will eat a Clouser Deep Minnow.

I really like using poppers and sliders, and of all the surface patterns, the Dahlberg Diver is my favorite. This spun deer hair fly can be tied to resemble many baitfish species, with a shaped head that makes the fly push water, pop and dive when stripped. The sound draws fish in close where they can track the fly by its wake. Often they crush it on top when it pauses.

So many flies, so little fishing time. I suggest you pick a few patterns you like and perfect their actions. With a handful of patterns, you can catch just about any inshore gamefish that swims, no matter how big. SB

Crab Flies

Spun deer hair fly can be tied to resemble many baitfish species, with a shaped head that makes the fly push water, pop and dive when stripped.

There are even flies designed to imitate crabs or brown shrimp. Crab flies are used to target specific gamefish like redfish, permit, tarpon and bonefish, since juicy crabs are among their primary prey. Most crab patterns are weighted so they sink to the bottom.

Often they can be worked higher in the water column until a fish spots the fly, and then the retrieve is stopped completely so the fly will fall to the bottom much like a live crab hoping to find cover or bury itself in the sand.

Other crab patterns are worked slowly over the bottom and allowed to remain motionless for a moment or two, and then hopped or scuttled along like a crab looking for a place to burrow. In either case, these flies are deadly. SB

CHAPTER 9

Reading the
Water

The mark of a successful fisherman is the ability to look at the water and have a sense of where the fish will be. The ability to read the water is imperative to fishing success. Knowing where changes in the bottom contour, the presence of structure or subtle changes in the current take place will help determine where the fish will hold and feed.

That ability to read the water is developed over time, and is the combination of remembering where you see and catch fish, as well as what your lures and baits do when put into those locations. As you learn more about the water you'll develop an innate sense of where things should be, and how your lure or bait should act when it lands there.

You'll find a good pair of polarized sunglasses goes a long way toward allowing you to see into the water and determine what lies beneath the surface. You'll also learn that the same things you can spot on your home waters will be present in other areas you fish. So let's discuss some of the consistencies we find when reading most inshore waters.

Fishing shallow means adopting a habit of the blue heron: Watch for fish movement.

See DVD for more on reading the water.

Working the edge of a spartina marsh during high tide. That's when redfish "root and snuffle" back in the grass, searching for crabs and other choice items. Wading and kayaking are two fine options for reaching shallow fish.

Learn to Avoid the Rough Spots

I f you want to be a successful inshore fisherman, it certainly helps to be able to read the water for signs of fish. It's actually easier than you think; as you find and catch fish, you learn to look for the same conditions, repeat scenarios from the good days. Almost anyone

There are a couple of basic tips when reading the water, and these will help you find fish, as well as avoid potential trouble.

can learn the little nuances that make a fishing spot good or bad—but if you really want to learn how to read the water, you're going to need a good pair of polarized glasses.

I never realized how important those glasses were for fishing, until I was a lifeguard on several Southeast Florida beaches. All day long the guard sitting next to me could spot schools of fish that I couldn't see, or at least never spotted until he pointed them out. After returning from a swim I mistakenly put on his glasses, and said to a third guard, "Look at that school of bluefish." His reply: "What school?" It was a big lesson.

There are a couple of basic tips when reading the water, and these will help you find fish, as well as avoid getting into trouble with your boat. In clear, salty coastal waters, for instance, a light brown or yellow color to the water is bad, as it usually means the water is very shallow. Green or blue means the water has some depth. If you know this, you can ease out onto a grassflat during a clean tide and spot both shallow and deep areas. Even more important, you can see contours on the bottom.

These contours are important because they mark bottom highways fish utilize as they move during tidal changes. If you're in a boat, they determine where your boat can go and

Different bottoms, different depths. These three boats are fishing between oyster bars (top), on very shallow grassflats mixed with sand bottom (middle) and in uniformly deeper water (bottom) using an electric motor to ease up on gamefish.

> Hunting for bigger reds and many other species means keeping a sharp eye, watching for potholes, sandbars and dropoffs.

what route you should take to intercept fish. At low tide, a school of bonefish might move out from the shallows and into a deeper hole or (broader bight) to avoid detection and predators. As the tide returns, fish may push out of the hole, maybe at first along a small channel only slightly deeper than the surrounding area—until the entire flat is flooded enough for the school to move around at will.

As gamefish and baitfish move along each

shallow, which explained why I caught only juveniles (rat reds) that were small enough to reach those areas. It was another lesson learned.

Hunting for bigger reds and many other species means keeping a sharp eye, watching for potholes, sandbars and dropoffs. Potholes in the grass appear as lighter areas, as do sandbars. Dropoffs have water that changes color, if the wind isn't blowing too hard and churning

Fishing extreme shallows requires patience, timing, stealth, finesse, and recognition of color and bottom differences. Good spotting and casting skills don't hurt, either. If you're going to spot shallow-water bonefish, left, redfish bottom left, or schooling stripers, opposite top, you will need polarized glasses. After all, you have to know which end of the fish to cast to, right?

flat, they often create wakes or push up their tails. These are clues you can look for. Redfish are famous for their tailing behavior, often in extreme shallows. But in some areas, the bigger ones are in somewhat deeper water, where they can move around effectively. Early in my fishing career, I'd been pursuing them in water too

Studying the water around a submerged sandbar, anglers are staked out and waiting for a sign. The tide may have to be just right before fish finally appear.

go from light to dark colors as the bottom materials change.

Reading the water is an essential element to consistent surf catches, particularly for school fish like pompano, bluefish and striped bass. Along the beaches, sandbars, troughs, rips and eddies form and change on a regular basis, something a salty surf veteran can judge with a moment's glance, and make his plans accordingly. For instance, pompano like to roam the back side of a sandbar during low tides. Stripers feed along the edges of current rips, and bluefish prefer to work the upcurrent side of a trough. With this little bit of knowledge, you can drive along the beach until you find that perfect sandbar, rip or trough.

things up. Where the two colors mix is likely the edge where predators lurk.

Knowing how to read the water will also reveal different bottom components. A bar with sand or shell bottom may trickle off into an area of mud bottom, very appealing to winter fish on a warm sunny day. Those areas

Essentially, your ability to read the water lets you put together pretty big pieces of the puzzle to catching fish with greater frequency. SB

Fish face into the current, and artificial lures moving against that current may be entirely shunned.

Fishing the Current

Along with different bottom contours, you'll want to take notice of the current speed and direction. It's not always as easy as it sounds, particularly when it's windy and there's a chop running. During these times you'll need a stationary object to determine the speed and direction of the water's movement, perhaps an old piling. Or, watch for drifting seaweed passing left to right, or vice versa.

Watch a stationary object to determine speed and direction of the current.

Current speed will determine how fast your lure or bait moves through a desired area, or how much weight you'll need to keep that bait on bottom. It's also important to understand your drift when in a boat, and which way the fish will be facing. (Upcurrent, of course.)

Knowing this, a lure or bait should be cast upcurrent and be allowed to move naturally with the tidal flood. Moving currents bring the groceries, and fish spend their entire lives waiting for food to arrive with the tides. Food moving in the wrong direction is more likely to be shunned than eaten, as fish find it unnatural.

Knowing the current's speed is important because it determines your boat's or bait's drift through a given area. Currents generally move quicker in deep water, with the exception of very shallow areas, where a buildup of water may be sheeted across.

Reading and judging the current reveals many things: if you need to set the anchor (and how much scope to use), whether to rig a sea anchor to slow the drift, or how fast you'll need to run a trolling motor. It's also a deciding factor in lure selection. In heavy currents, you may need to utilize a lure with a big lip or heavy weight to get down to the fish. SB

CHAPTER 10

Understanding Tidal Influence

If you're going to fish inshore waters, it's imperative you understand the tides; they will affect your success and safety. The gravitational pull of the sun and moon have tremendous impacts on the feeding and movements of inshore gamefish. Fish sense the major and minor changes in the tides and react accordingly, so by knowing when these changes take place, you can anticipate their actions.

Tides usually play a role in your fishing success. They affect the movement of natural food items like shrimp, crabs and minnows. Tides expose and cover a lot of coastal bottom, providing fish access to sandbars and flats. Tides also allow fish to spread out over a large area, or concentrate them in one location.

As an angler, you should learn how tides impact inshore fish you have an interest in. Over time, you'll find these fish are creatures of habit, and that conditions during a specific tide will often reoccur on that same tide phase in the future. To learn more about tides and the roles they play in fishing, turn the page and let's get started.

Keep a tide chart handy around the house; it can make all the difference in the world.

See DVD for more on tidal influence.

Low tide? No problem—if you know where the deeper holes are where fish congregate when water becomes scarce.

A Changing of the Tides

f you think about it, the feeding habits of most fish can be attributed to the direction and flow of tides. It's tides that drive the forage and control the comfort for most fish species. It's the tides that determine where fish hold in a given location and which direction they face.

The bite today might be on an incoming tide, and that might be related to a school of small minnows that's swept into the feeding zone by the incoming water. At another time, the outgoing tide might sweep shrimp into an area and that sets up the bite. A low tide might force fish out of the spartina grass and into a creekmouth, or a high tide might let those same fish forage up against a shoreline. Tidal influence is a contributing factor to

Tidal influence is a contributing factor to virtually all fish habitats.

virtually all fish habits.

Wind is the contributing factor that can hold up or accentuate tidal movement. If these tides coincide with extreme wind that flows in the same direction as the tidal movement, then you get the amazing tides that drive food out of their normal safety zones and send fish into feeding frenzies.

You'll want to know when spring tides are taking place, because the extreme low tidal ranges can leave you and your boat high and dry in a spot you fished during the low tide only a week earlier. Besides being embarrassing to watch your boat tilt over onto dry land, if you get caught high and dry just before dark, you can easily transform from predator to prey when the mosquitoes move in for supper.

These same low tides can be used to your advantage because they concentrate fish and food. If you fish a Texas flat that is several miles long, an extreme low will make that flat get very skinny, forcing all the larger gamefish

Sun-Moon Tides

Tides are a function of the gravitational pull of the moon and sun, and to a lesser extent the force of the wind. The stronger the gravitational pull of the moon, the greater the tide in most situations. Lunar gravitational pull is greatest when the moon is in a new or full phase, which is when the sun and moon line up with the Earth. The tides that take place during the new and full moons are called spring tides, even though they take place all year long. Spring tides encourage tidal extremes—higher than normal high tides and lower than normal low tides. These extremes really drive the fish wild. The current moves a lot of food that normally doesn't come their way or concentrates that forage in one location. A lot of the annual spawning runs for shrimp, crabs and finfish take place during the extremes of the spring tides.

As a rule, the spring tides that take place during the spring months have lower low tides than normal, while the spring tides that occur in the fall promote higher than normal high tides. SB

Above, snook are ambush feeders that feed best on strong tides. Opposite, angler fishing a spring tide riser for prowling redfish.

In some spots, it takes a slack tide to allow bait to remain in one location long enough for fish to eat. Especially while inlet fishing.

to move to deeper water. That may mean a deep hole somewhere on that flat, but more often it means the edges of the flat where the area drops off to deeper water. You can wade those dropoffs and sometimes crush the trout and reds.

Extreme low tides are a good time to take notice of characteristics of a flat that you don't normally see. When flats dry up, only the deepest areas hold water, and they're very obvious. Take notice of those spots, and you'll

Exposed sticks with dark water lines means that the tide is low. Use caution when navigating.

Tides on the Rocks

Sometimes fish will bite on a slack tide. One example is when gamefish have bait concentrated and remain in a feeding frenzy while the tide changes. In other spots, fish are in areas where the current is so strong, it takes a slack tide to allow bait to remain in one location long enough for fish to eat.

You see the latter situation quite a bit when fishing inlets for mangrove snapper. The snapper have to sit so close to the rocks during fast tides, that it's hard to get a bait to them. When the tide starts to slacken, fish can move away from the rocks to feed. As the tide goes totally slack, it's a lot easier to get a bait in front of them. Unfortunately there's a very short window of slack tide for this situation. SB

Highs and Lows

know where the fish are likely to move on lesser tides when there's still plenty of water for the fish to remain on the flat. Those same areas are the first places a school of redfish or bonefish will hunt as they move back onto the flat with the incoming tide.

Extreme high tides bring a lot of water flow through inlets and into rivers and bays. They bring clean, clear, ocean or gulf water inshore. A large portion of the gamefish that move from the beaches to the inshore waters push in with these tides. That brings outstanding fishing around inlets, rivermouths and other areas with deep water and strong tidal exchange. A lot of bait that migrates from near-shore waters to the inshore waters (such as during the fall mullet run that takes place on the east coast), do so on these tides.

A wind that opposes the tidal direction will limit the effect of the tide and thus limit the food being swept into a given area. It may take a day or so for the wind to noticeably affect the tidal range, but prolonged winds from the same direction can really throw the tide ranges off even during spring tides. You might see flats go completely dry, or high tides where the water comes over the top of the docks.

Neap tides take place during half moon phases and reflect a weak or normal tidal range. There will still be strong tides when the wind and tide are moving in the same direction after the wind has been blowing in that direction for several days, but of nowhere near the strength and water flow of spring tides. The nice thing about neap tides is their consistency. You're certainly less likely to get caught by a low tide and run aground on a flat during a neap tide.

The keys to fishing tides are in learning when they take place, and how they affect local bait and gamefish populations. What you'll learn over time is that tidal influences play a key role in these movements, and allow you to better target fish. By paying attention to the smaller details of tides, you'll learn to use them to your advantage. SB

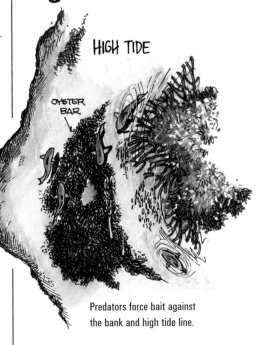

Predators force bait against the bank and high tide line.

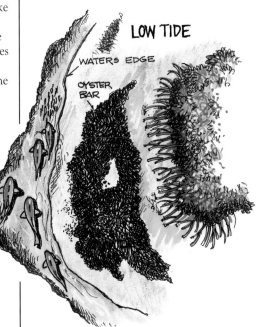

Lower water depth exposes bar and forces the fish to seek deeper water near a point. Fish will return with the incoming tide.

CHAPTER 11

Weather Plays a Role

Just as the changes in weather affect your life, they have a role in the feeding and movement of fish. In fact, fish have the ability to sense the changes in temperature and barometric pressure better than anglers. What you'll find is that weather influences tides, water depth and clarity, as well as the comfort of inshore gamefish.

The nice thing about weather is that it often follows a pattern. By learning how fish react to weather, you will see patterns develop for their movements and feeding habits. You'll soon find that the barometer and thermometer can be your best fishing indicators, and that overcast skies can certainly prolong the bite.

Wind can speed up or kill tides, and it can stack water along the shoreline or hold it back from exiting an inshore bay or lagoon for prolonged periods. Winds also affect the temperature, so the two go hand-in-hand when determining what weather is doing to your fishing.

Let's take a look at different weather patterns, and those little nuances and how they play a role in when and where fish feed. It soon become easy to see patterns that affect the fish near you.

Barometric pressure is a function of weather patterns and fish can detect these changes.

Boat scampers for the boat ramp and safety, as threatening weather looms. Old-timers call this cloud formation "witches tails," and it means sudden high winds, rain and possible waterspouts. Below, the payoff for a picture-perfect morning.

Picking the Right Weather

About 10 years ago I went fishing in Homosassa, Florida with a guide who drove us down a long, winding river and out into the open Gulf of Mexico. We weaved around flats of solid limestone and worked into a small depression in the rocks where he killed the engine and set out the anchor. I picked up a rod and started casting. He picked up a sand-wich and started eating. After about 15 min-utes without success I asked my guide if maybe we ought to move to another spot. He put down his sandwich and said something I'll always remember, "You can keep on casting, but the fish aren't going to bite until the wind goes south."

Dumbfounded by the statement, I had to know more, and he obliged my interest.

"When the wind shifts to the south, that'll drop the barometer, and the fish will go on the feed. I looked at the weather before we left, and that should take place in about 30 minutes."

Sure as rain on my day off, in 30 minutes the wind shifted to the south, and a few minutes later I was into the best redfish bite I'd ever experienced. Since that day, I've tried to moni-tor the barometer whenever I plan to get out on the water.

Barometric pressure is a function of weather patterns. Fish can detect these changes through the lateral lines in their bodies, or so some fish-ermen say. As a fish goes from fry to adult, it learns over time that certain pressures indicate weather changes that might limit the ability to find and catch prey, so they start to search out food with reckless abandon at the first sign of these changes.

Depending on where in the country you live, the most consistent weather patterns will take place at a different time of year. Where I live in Stuart, Florida, which is on the southeastern coast of the state, I know the seatrout are going to feed when a winter cold front hits Tallahassee, up around the state capitol. That's about eight hours before the frontal line reach-es Stuart.

These fronts normally come through every four to six days in winter, and I can tell just by

The unfortunate side of weather is that it is still very unpredictable.

Fishing during summer, when (mostly) afternoon thunderstorms can be severe, can be a little tricky.

More beautiful weather, with a thin, see-through shower in the background that offers no threat.

looking at the weather if I need to target seatrout, or go after another species. What you need to do is figure out when that change in barometer takes place in your hometown, and use it to your advantage. And don't think seatrout are the only species affected. Striped

shallows into water a few feet deeper as the sun comes up, or look for areas that provide shade like docks or boat houses.

Conversely, overcast may encourage fish to remain in the shallows or actively hunt in those areas. Fish that normally move off the

Wind is a huge factor. More often than not, it's better to have less wind than more—everyone knows that. The rules can change, however.

bass, redfish, pompano, snook, tarpon and bonefish all follow certain feeding patterns as major weather systems progress.

Sunlight, rain and wind all have major influences on gamefish. Many fish seem to react to the angle of the sun. As it climbs over the horizon, fish may move to deeper water to escape the rays shining in their eyes. Warming water may also compel them to seek cooler depths. Knowing this, an angler can move from the

Sunny conditions are fine for bay fishing, generally before 11 a.m. After that, the fish may very well turn off.

flats during the heat of the day now feed actively on those flats all day long.

The opposite applies to the cold weather months when the angle of the sun is low. On sunny days, fish move onto the flats in the afternoon when the sun has heated the water. On the cloudy days, they'll stay in the deeper holes because they are warmer. Then again, not all fish follow these patterns. The point is, for each species and region, there are patterns to watch for. Learn how weather affects your favorite target fish and you can better pick your days.

Wind is a huge factor. More often than not, it's better to have less wind than more wind. But there are exceptions. When I was in my early 20s and had just started snook fishing, I knew there was a select group of the best snook anglers (I called them Sharpies) that I watched for every time I drove over a bridge. If I saw more than two members of the group on the bridge I knew the fishing was good.

Inside this group of about 20 anglers were five or six men that only targeted trophy fish. What amazed me about the group was how consistent they were. If they showed up on a bridge, the big fish were sure to be there. What I also learned was that this group always ended up on a certain bridge when the wind was howling out of the north and the tide was moving in the same direction. A north wind over 20 miles per hour and outgoing tide meant the big snook were going to be feeding around the bridges, and these guys had it pegged. When they showed up, you

Inlet fishing can be high-charged and exciting, especially during rough and windy conditions.

can bet the local snook population took a hit.

In most cases heavy winds limit fishing areas and dirties up the water, making it harder to find and target inshore gamefish. Roiled water may take several days or even weeks to clean up. Given a choice, I'll take zero wind over lots of wind any day of the week.

That being said, there is always some lee (protected) area that can be fished on windy days. Fishing in the lee allows for better casting and working of a lure or bait. If you have to fish heavy winds and are out in a boat, a drift sock or even a 5-gallon bucket tied off to a spring cleat will slow the boat enough to allow for some sense of consistency with each cast.

Weather is probably of most concern to surf fishermen. Pressure changes create waves, literally. As fronts move through, changes in pressure along with wind speed and direction determine the surf that will bombard that stretch of coastline. Choppy surf can be good for fishing. Baitfish may get caught up in the foam and moving water, confused, making them easy prey for fish like striped bass and tarpon. On the other hand, waves may be so big and out of control that it completely eliminates any opportunity to fish.

Wind direction on the beach controls the drift or longshore current, the current that runs parallel to the shoreline. A hard wind parallel to the shoreline will push the water in the same direction. Too much of that can be bad, because it limits your ability to hold bottom

with weights and forces seagrasses to collect on the line. It can also be a good thing because it can push a lot of bait into the troughs and deeper holes inside the bars, attracting predatory fish close to shore. The key here is to know the limitations of the wind and currents along with the feeding habits of the fish.

The unfortunate side of weather is that it's still very unpredictable. But if you monitor the weather closely, you'll find that very specific patterns develop that you'll be able to use to find these inshore fish. Any time you can actually predict where and when fish will eat, you *really* help your odds of finding them and having an exceptional day on the water. SB

To slow your boat's drift on a breezy day, trying using a sea anchor, or drift sock.

CHAPTER 12

Structure

Nature appreciates structure. Fish, crabs, worms, baitfish and all sorts of marine life interact around structure. It provides food and sanctuary, and a temporary home where inshore gamefish find comfort and protection. Some fish use structure for shade, others to ambush passing prey. Whatever the reason, it's just a better place to fish than open water.

Good fishing structure may be obvious or subtle. It might be a local rockpile or section of reef. The pilings of docks, piers and bridges are prime, as are seawalls and bulkheads. Submerged trees and rocks hold their share of fish, since they provide a break in the current. Sunken boats make great structure for a variety of fish, but a floating boat, either docked or anchored, may hold fish in the heat of the day.

Structure can be as subtle as an old barbeque grill that someone threw in the bay down in South Florida. Someone figured out that a dozen slot-size snook were holding on the downcurrent side of the grill, waiting to ambush mullet. Once they figured it out, it was a simple task to ease up quietly, fire a live mullet at the grill, and wait for the strike.

Learn the best fish-attracting structures in your area, for consistent action.

See DVD for more on fishing structure.

Working a mangrove shoreline early in the morning is a good bet for trophy trout or snook. Below, certain docks in the bay earn a reputation as fish attractors. Why fish prefer some docks over others remains a mystery.

Structures Big and Small

I f there's been one inherent theme to this book, it's that inshore gamefish and their forage are structure oriented. In open water, anything under 100 pounds at one time or

Earnest anglers on a beach pier: it's a mackerel school.

another can be considered as...bait. A fish swimming in open water had better be the largest predator in the area. If not, it could be in jeopardy at some point.

The importance of structure is twofold—it presents a place to hide and a place to hunt. It's that simple. Even the smallest marine life, like shrimp, are attracted to structure for protection and the food it offers. Mullet feed on the different algae growing on rocks and docks, and they use those same places to elude larger predators.

Flounder are attracted to bridge pilings because they block the current flow, which in turn attracts small minnows and other baitfish feeding in the eddy. Flounder also use that sand or mud bottom as camouflage and ease up to the pilings to feed on small fish. If a shark is lurking nearby, flounder shuffle closer to the pilings, hoping to remain unnoticed, or at least make it tougher for a shark to approach.

It all boils down to structure, but there are so many different types of structure out there. Probably the best fish attractors are the natural spots like sandbars, reefs and oyster bars. Also various seagrasses, like turtlegrass. And don't forget spartina, the most important of all shoreline marsh grasses. Mangrove trees also offer coastline protection not only to fish, but coastal residents. These types of structure attract fish because they are building blocks for the food chain and regularly hold food items of all sizes. The smallest "critters" attract bigger ones, which in turn attract the top predators.

Man-made structures like docks, bridges, piers and artificial reefs also attract their share of gamefish, but it takes time for these structures to build up a healthy coating of barnacles and oysters. Let's look at the different types of structure individually.

Sandbars

These are formed by wind, waves and tide. Along the edges of those bars are crabs and different mollusks. Atop the bars are shrimp,

Redfish and trout prowl the sandbar's edge.

Trees and Forests

Trees (alive or dead) offer protection and a place to hunt prey. In southern Florida, the natural decaying matter produced by falling mangrove leaves feeds the smallest marine organisms, which in turn draw shrimp and crabs to the areas. Snook, snapper, redfish and even 100-pound tarpon all hunt the mangrove forest edges, hoping to scare grocery items into open water, where they're easier to catch. For you, the trick to catching is to cast directly to the roots and work the bait back into the open, though not far from the trees. Gamefish know most baitfish and shrimp aren't going to venture far from the trees; it's not natural. Too far out, and gamefish often give up pursuit.

clams and other bivalves. It's a regular smorgasbord of tasty food items. Striped bass, weakfish, flounder, pompano, whiting and croaker regularly hunt for food over the tops of sandbars during high water. During low water, the

Wading the sandbars and flats, looking for bonefish. Ahead is the quarry...

mobile food chain is forced to the edges, where even larger fish like sharks, permit, tarpon and other species can take advantage.

When fishing around sandbars, you can expect some gamefish to move on top of the

bar to feed during those higher tide phases. Other fish like snook, for instance, will still hunt the edges of the bar for food being swept over the dropoff. As the tide recedes, lack of water forces these fish from the top of the bar, so the best areas to fish are the dropoffs and nearby channel edges. One of the most effective ways to fish these areas is to wade the sandbar and cast upcurrent and parallel to the bar, working the lure or bait back along the entire dropoff. A lot of bigger gamefish are sitting in a little deeper water but come up onto the bar to seize that easy meal.

Reefs and Rocks

Natural reefs come in many forms of material, from coquina rock, oolitic limestone to coral. Living reefs contain their own organisms that attract smaller marine life seeking food, but also safety in the rocks. The most attractive reef areas have a lot of growth on them, either in the form of

You figure these snook are hanging around jetty rocks for their health? Actually they are; it's that food and shelter thing again.

"live rock," or of natural algae and other marine plants. Starfish, urchins, crabs, lobsters and different mollusks hang around the reef. Some of them end up on the dinner table themselves.

Fishing here may require a controlled technique of dropping the bait down, and reeling it up several turns on the reel, so that it remains several feet above structure. Let out too much line, and a live bait will surely seek those rocks for cover, which means snagging tackle. Suspending a bait over the structure allows bait to remain active in the strike zone, yet close enough to structure that it still looks natural.

Shallow reefs and rockpiles allow anglers to cast floating/diving plugs and reel them over the top of the structure so the lure swims among the rocks, but not in them so there's no danger of snagging the rocks. Live baitfish like mullet can be fished this way as well, but with close attention to the movements of the baitfish. If it makes a beeline for the rocks, it needs to be reeled out immediately.

A lot of fish—snook, striped bass, snappers and tautog—hunt the edges of reefs and rocks without entering these structures. At times they move into the reef to seek protection, but when hunting they prefer the edge where they hold tight to the rocks and ambush any food that happens by. For these species, live baits or lures (like a jig) are very effective when worked on the sandy side of the reef and parallel to the structure.

Oyster Reefs

Oyster bars are natural areas for gamefish to congregate, because they often allow the tide to direct water and food. Worms, crabs and other food items live among the oysters, and various fish like red drum, seatrout and snook hunt there. The oysters, however, are cruelly

sharp and catch just about any lure or bait even near them. The trick to fishing these reefs is to work the mud edges, instead of the reef tops. Watch for zones which increase the water flow and pull baitfish along it. Cast upcurrent of

Angler above plumbs the oyster beds for fish. That guy below is hooked up with a good one, while fly-casting in the marsh.

these areas and work the bait with the flow. Weedless lures like gold spoons, spinnerbaits and jerkbaits are excellent choices around the oysters.

Marsh and Grass

If you fish the coastal marshes of Georgia or the Carolinas, you're likely familiar with oysters and spartina (cord) grass. When the tides flood the marsh up onto the grass, these areas are natural fish attractors. Small baitfish like finger mullet, minnows and shrimp all move into the grass for safety and to feed. Redfish and seatrout are right on their tails.

People Places

Man-made structures like docks, bridges and piers are extremely effective at attracting marine life. As the pilings gather growth they also attract food, which brings in gamefish. Sheepshead want that steady supply of food hiding among the oysters growing on pilings. Tautog love those small green crabs that live in the nooks and crannies. Small baitfish use pilings to get out of the current and feed on drifting plankton—but they're the food that draws the gamefish.

These structures get a coating of marine growth within a few months. They offer a place to hide and shelter from the current.

The thin strands of spartina would be easy to fish if they weren't so thick and intertwined. The best way to fish spartina is to work the open water edges, or wait until a falling tide pulls water from an obvious washout. Fish the

mouth of the washout where seatrout, sheepshead, flounder and redfish gather. Live shrimp under corks and jerkbaits are the common options around spartina, but that doesn't mean other weedless baits like spoons, jigs and other soft plastics aren't effective.

Probably the most common and thus most effective type of structure you'll encounter are bottom seagrasses. Quite a few marine organisms live and feed on the grasses themselves, and just about every juvenile gamefish species utilizes grass bottom to hide from larger predators. The largest gamefish utilize sand holes in the grass as ambush points where they can seize food out in the open. Grasses grow only so tall,

and many will allow you to work a lure or live bait directly over the top of the grass bed, using the countdown method we talked about earlier. You can also focus on casting to potholes and working around the sand patches. If the grass grows all the way to the surface, a weedless lure is a must—and that's when a gold spoon or jerkbait will really shine, so to speak.

Artificial Reefs

Man-made reefs are another good source of structure, often badly needed in empty areas, and they're built in many forms. They make artificial reefs out of a host of different materials, with concrete forms or pipes being the favorite, legal material. These structures get a coating of marine growth within a few months. Reefs provide a lot of protection in open water, and offer a place to hide and rest from the current. Gamefish gather too, many seeking a rest from the current, waiting for food to drift past.

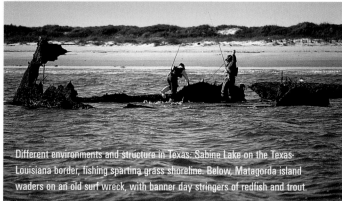

Different environments and structure in Texas: Sabine Lake on the Texas-Louisiana border, fishing spartina grass shoreline. Below, Matagorda island waders on an old surf wreck, with banner day stringers of redfish and trout.

The most effective way to fish these structures is to use a bait or lure that bounces along or just above bottom. Try jigs or lipped swimming plugs, and weighted baits like a shrimp and jig combination. Or maybe a live eel or baitfish on a fishfinder bottom rig. All are deadly around this type of structure. The larger artificial reefs can be fished just like natural reefs, by keeping a bait above or to the side of the structure.

So you see, everything in salt water hangs around structure. It's up to you to fish it effectively, and you do that by learning the feeding habits of your quarry.

Remember, fish out in the open may be just bait for something else, while fish around structure feel safe enough to feed. SB

CHAPTER 13

Knowledge of
Knots

Your ability to cast, hook and land fish is completely dependent on the knots you choose. Options are plentiful: Smaller knots that fit easily through the rod guides allow for longer casts, while a hook attached with a snell knot might have a better hook-up ratio than a loop knot. That so-called 100 percent knot will likely help you land more fish.

There are pretty knots and easy knots, but the best are those you tie with confidence and efficiency on a regular basis. It's actually better to pick out just a handful of knots and learn them well. Learn to tie them well and quickly under all conditions, even in the dark.

The more you tie these knots, the easier they'll be to whip out when the fish are biting fast and furious.

Practice a few of these knots, and you'll likely increase your catch rate.

The simple loop knot adds
action and wiggle to lures and
jigs that lack built-in action.

Using the Double Line

As a writer, I get to fish with some top captains in the country. It's a benefit of the job that I get to learn from people who have dedicated their lives to one fish, or one style of fishing. From television personali-

Author wisely used a double line while catching this huge tarpon. An ounce of prevention...

ties to fishing guides, the one intangible that I've noticed among this group of the nation's best is their attention to knots.

The best anglers tie knots that are easy and quick to master, have a high tensile strength and don't come loose under extreme pressure. I'm a stickler for good knots, and I only tie a handful of them to keep up my consistency. If I were to pick the one knot that should be in every saltwater angler's arsenal, it would be the Bimini twist. There are two good knots for producing a double line above a leader—the Bimini Twist and the spider hitch, which is a

Those fish wouldn't have been landed had I been lazy and not rigged up with a Bimini twist.

good knot for light line or braided lines, but doesn't hold up as well with lines over 12-pound test.

Why start off doubling your fishing line? First off, the Bimini twist is a 100 percent knot, which means it equals the breaking strength of the line without a knot. Forego this step and the knot you tie between fishing line and leader will be the weak link. A properly tied double line ensures maximum strength at this crucial interface.

Secondly, during the course of a long fight, fish like tarpon, cobia and other large inshore gamefish will strike the line repeatedly with their tails. Over time, they can abrade the line. I can't tell you how many times I've reeled in a fish with one of the strands of the double line broken. That's a fish I would have lost had I not used a double-line knot. And it's always a quality fish. Over the course of a year, I probably land 30 or more big fish that have one of these strands of double line broken. Those fish wouldn't have been landed had I been lazy and not rigged up with a Bimini twist. That adds up quickly.

Once you have a double line knot secured, you'll have to decide what knot you want to use to join the line to leader. In most saltwater fishing a small shock or bite leader is used, between the standing line and the lure or bait. In most cases, it's used for abrasion resistance, but in some it's used to control fish close to the boat. A favorite amoung many anglers for tying double line to leader is the uni-knot.

At the terminal end of the leader I like to use a loop-style knot when connecting lures or hooks. The advantage of a loop knot is that the loop allows the hook or lure to swing freely,

Bimini Twist

Once learned, it can be tied in less than a minute.

1 Double the end of your line, making the doubled portion about three feet long. Insert your hand in the loop and make 20 complete revolutions with your hand to form the 20 wraps. Note that at this stage, the wraps are spread over a considerable portion of the line.

The one most important thing to remember when tying the Bimini is to keep constant pressure on all three points.

2 Sitting erect, hold your knees tightly together and place the loop over them. Maintain pressure, as shown, with your hands on both the standing line and the short end.

3 Spread your knees slowly, maintaining very tight hand pressure in opposing directions, as before. This will draw the wraps tightly together.

4 Once the wraps are very snug, pull slightly downward with the short end while relaxing tension slightly at the same time. Be sure to keep up the tension, however, with the left hand and with the knees.

5 The line should then roll easily over the wraps, all the way down to the end.

6 Completed rollover before it is anchored with a half-hitch around one strand, and several half hitches around both strands.

7 This shows detail of finishing half hitches: the first around a single strand, and three others around both strands. Instead of making three separate finishing hitches, you can make just one—and go through it three times with the tag end instead of only once. Trim, leaving about an eighth-inch end.

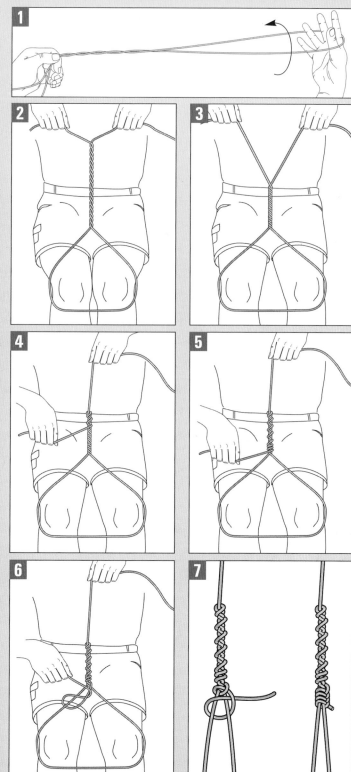

The Uni-Knot System

Familiarize yourself with the simple procedure of using the uni-knot here and then all other uni-knot applications (line to line, line to leader, leader to hook and loop knot) become quite easy.

Turn the end back toward the eye to form a circle.

With thumb and finger of the left hand, grasp both strands of line and the crossing strand in a single grip just forward of the hook.

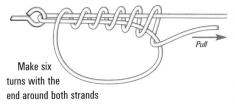

Pull

Make six turns with the end around both strands of line and through the circle. (With light lines—say 2- to 12-pound test—you should make five or six turns. If using heavier line, four turns will be sufficient).

Pull here to snug up the knot

Maintaining the same grip with the left hand, pull on the end of the line in the direction shown by the arrow until all the wraps are snugged tight and close together. Snugging down tightly at this stage is essential to maximum knot strength.

Trim

Pull line to draw the knot down to the eye

Finally, slide the finished knot tight against the eye of the hook by dropping the tag end and pulling solely on the standing part of the line. The excess end can be trimmed flush with the knot after final positioning.

imparting more action to the lure or bait. Again the uni-knot can be used to create a loop in the line as well.

Another good knot to know is the dropper loop. This knot can be used to tie a series of different surf and bottom rigs. I use the dropper loop for everything from pompano to mutton snapper, and even use it to tie jigs in tandem for trout fishing.

It's also a good idea to know how to snell a hook. Hooks that have turned-down eyes are becoming more popular these days, and they're the easiest and best style to snell. Snelling a hook will hold the leader in a straight line with the hook for a more positive hookset. A lot of circle hooks and other livebait hooks on the market today have eyes turned down or up, and they can be either snelled or tied with a loop

Line to Line Uni-Knot

Tying line to line is actually done the same way as tying line to hook, even though the two parallel strands involved are from different pieces of line.

It can be increased to 100 percent if you double both strands of line before tying the pair of uni-knots, but the single tie is strong enough for all practical purposes, and is trimmer.

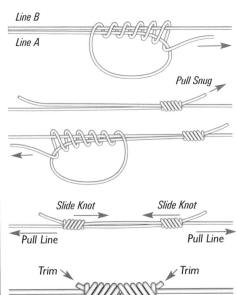

Line B

Line A

Pull Snug

Slide Knot *Slide Knot*

Pull Line *Pull Line*

Trim *Trim*

knot for the best hook-set ratio.

As an angler, you'll gravitate to a handful of your favorite knots, the ones you have the most confidence in. Extra care and patience in knot-tying will pay dividends over the years. You'll land fish that other weaker or poorly tied knots would have lost.

The uni system will be enough to get you through most applications, but if you want to learn other popular knots Florida Sportsman's *Complete Book of Baits, Rigs and Tackle* by Vic Dunaway is a great source for these knots and more.

Uni-Knot Loop

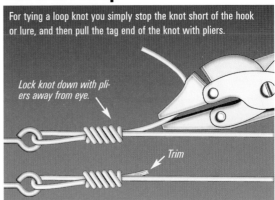

For tying a loop knot you simply stop the knot short of the hook or lure, and then pull the tag end of the knot with pliers.

Lock knot down with pliers away from eye.

Trim

Spider Hitch

This knot has often been touted as a good alternative to the Bimini twist, especially when using braided fishing lines. But there really is no good alternative. The spider hitch often tests at 100 percent on a machine, but gradually weakens during a long fight, while the Bimini does not.

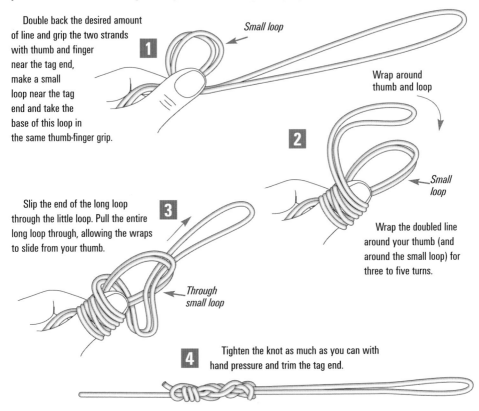

Double back the desired amount of line and grip the two strands with thumb and finger near the tag end, make a small loop near the tag end and take the base of this loop in the same thumb-finger grip.

1

Small loop

Wrap around thumb and loop

2

Small loop

Wrap the doubled line around your thumb (and around the small loop) for three to five turns.

Slip the end of the long loop through the little loop. Pull the entire long loop through, allowing the wraps to slide from your thumb.

3

Through small loop

4 Tighten the knot as much as you can with hand pressure and trim the tag end.

CHAPTER 14

Safety

There's no substitute for safety on the water. It's the safe and sound decisions that make for a good day on the water.

Even when you make good decisions, there is always the unexpected that may pop up, simply by stepping into the marine environment. The protective spines of stingrays, catfish and sea urchins commonly find their way into fishermen. Stinging jellyfish are also around, available in a variety of shapes, sizes and degrees of pain. Any time you're on the water you're exposing yourself to possible hypothermia or dehydration. There are also strange bacteria that thrive in the marine world that require close monitoring, if you should become exposed.

This doesn't mean you're likely to suffer some major injury while fishing. In fact, if you're careful and pay attention while on the water, you're very unlikely to become injured in any major way. With that said, this chapter looks at some of the more common marine injuries, with ways to avoid and treat them.

Pay attention, be prepared and take your time, and you'll have a safe day on the water.

See DVD for more on safety

There's no better way to mess up your day, than to step on a stingray while wadefishing. If you wear protective clothes and footwear while wading, it can save months of pain and discomfort.

Dodging the Sharp Stuff

nshore fishing is not all fun and games. You should approach your fishing day with a sharp mind, because if you're off your "A-Game" just a little and are handling toothy fish, your friends might forever call you Lefty, and it won't have *anything* to do with politics.

the flesh-eating kind), so what doesn't get you today might get you a few hours or days later.

The old Boy Scout motto, "Be Prepared" is especially true when fishing inshore waters. I carry a first aid kit on the boat and in my vehicle at all times. It's an invaluable tool that I've used for everything from stopping bleeding to patching loose reel seats. You won't need it often but when you do, it's really nice to have around.

A well-prepared mariner and fisherman knows how to deal with catfish or stingray

A variety of things can go wrong when handling fish with sharp hooks attached.

Any time you're handling live fish with hooks in them, there's a variety of things that can go wrong. From a fish that shakes loose from your grasp and drives a treble hook into your hand, to a stingray skulking on bottom that can be stepped on, marine injuries can be serious. Keep in mind that the marine environment is loaded with bacteria (occasionally

punctures, jellyfish stings, hypothermia, heat stroke, dehydration, impaled hooks, fish (usually catfish) spines, even major and minor cuts. Risk avoidance is the best policy, but sooner or later you'll have a situation.

Fin punctures from sea catfish are common enough, and some have even been treated by doctors. The same goes for stingrays. Both have a protein poison that can cause severe discomfort, though it can be alleviated some with fairly hot water. (Cook the protein, neutralize the poison). Unfortunately, spines are also exposed to the open marine environment and are typically laden with bacteria, so antibiotic treatment is recommended.

Jellyfish produce a neurotransmitter type of toxin that can send pain impulses throughout the body. The toxin is very close to that of a bee sting, only a more severe dose of the poison, which also triggers anaphylactic shock for those who are allergic. Severe encounters with jellyfish can attack your lymphatic system, and curl you up into a ball of pain. There are treatments on the market like Epi-Pen, which can counteract jellyfish stings, but the best topical treatment is a combination of alcohol and meat tenderizer. If the sting victim shows any signs of respiratory distress or more severe pain, you should seek immediate medical attention.

Hypothermia, heat stroke and dehydration are related to overexposure to the elements. Try to avoid these issues by dressing in layers in cold weather, and replenishing your liquids in warm weather. Numbness and lack of coordination are signs of hypothermia that should tell you it's time to get indoors. Or out of the water, at least, since it chills the body many times faster than air. Unfortunately, fishermen are lost every year this way. They wind up unexpectedly in water that is colder than they ever imagined, and lose their body heat before being rescued. Restoring that body heat means plenty of warm liquids and blankets. On the flip side during summer, profuse sweating and cold, clammy skin are classic signs of heat stroke, which can also be fatal. Lots of liquids, ice and even a quick dunk in the nearest water are advised, if it can safely be done. Both are extreme conditions to be avoided.

Getting Stuck

If you fish long enough, you can expect to get a hook through your skin. (The odds simply catch up with most anglers, though admittedly it happens more often with some). If the hook gets under your skin, you can use the field method of hook removal. That requires first cutting the line off at the hook. Carefully double some fishing line (or better yet, 40-pound mono leader) and loop it around the shank or curve of the hook, gripping the line with both hands. Have the person who is hooked push down on the hook eye so that it meets the skin. That helps clear the barb for removal. The helper gives a firm yank on the line and the hook pops out. Many people go right back to fishing afterward, none the worse for wear. The spot should be thoroughly cleaned with antibacterial wipes or soap, and perhaps covered, though it should be remembered that sunlight does kill bacteria. Using Neosporin later that evening on the wound works wonders, and often there is no soreness the next day. A tetanus shot every five years helps, too. Watch closely for signs of redness or soreness, which can mean infection.

If the hook point enters and exits the skin, push the hook all the way through so that the barb also exits the skin. Cut the hook behind the barb with wire cutters (you do have needlenose pliers and diagonal cutters on the boat, right?) and then back the hook out.

Cuts and scrapes of all kinds are also common with inshore fishing. I've cut myself wading barefoot and stepped on broken glass, slipped on jetty rocks and been shredded by barnacles, even had numerous fish bite and poke me. SB

Gripping fish properly is important. Cautious angler at top holds a bluefish behind the head. Sea catfish is held tight around poisonous spines. Striped bass and other sandpaper-mouthed species can be lipped.

Just wearing a quality pair of shoes is important. Plantar fasciitis is a common ailment with fishermen, caused by insufficient heel support and padding. The searing pain commonly lasts for months, and it's certainly worth buying good deck shoes with inexpensive, full footpad inserts. Cheap flip-

Anglers who wade all day should use high-top tennis shoes at the very least. Better yet, try wading shoes or boots and socks sturdy enough to deflect stingray spines or cruel oysters.

flops, leather docksider shoes and fishing barefoot on a hard surface are likely the three worst culprits that wear out fishermen's feet. As for fishing barefoot all the time, the possibilities for injury are far too numerous to mention here.

Getting poked or hurt is a common aspect of this sport, but if you're prepared with a good first aid kit, and wear a good hat, sun-proof clothing, sunglasses and good shoes, you can dodge tons of discomfort. Don't forget that 50 SPF sunscreen either; no reason to give your local skin doctor an excuse to carve on you in the future. SB

In Texas, where folks wadefish by the thousands, serious anglers gear up with no-nonsense neoprene waders and lace-on boots. A belt at the waist cinches the waders shut, in case of a sudden dunking. This couple is protected from hypothermia, stingrays, oyster cuts, sand abrasions and water-borne bacteria. The neoprene covering is an investment in comfort and safety. Nice equipment for stalking trophy trout.

CHAPTER 15

Conservation

Whether you catch a nice fish or not, and whether your kids and others who come along later have good fishing, depends a lot on one word: Conservation.

Sure, your skill and know-how are important. But the fish have to be there in the first place for you to catch them.

Anglers can play a huge role in protecting fish stocks, and growing them.

In the past we've had to suffer outrageous overfishing and mishandling of our fisheries. Fortunately, we've also seen landmark changes and positive gains that directly increase your successes.

By Florida Sportsman
Founder Karl Wickstrom

Fish are a public resource, and should be shared equally among all user groups.

Time for reflection on a quiet evening of wade fishing. Conservation of marine fish has been in the forefront for many years now, and anglers have won many battles. More remain in the future, something very much worth fighting for.

We Can Make A Big Difference

Anglers can be primary stewards of the resource and many have considered conservation issues their call to action. They've taken part in fisheries decisions on all levels. They've beaten City Hall, so to speak. In fact they've won some historic battles.

Let's always remember that our fisheries are a public resource that must be shared carefully and equally.

Veteran fishermen remember too well how commercial gill nets depleted fish stocks badly in coastal waters of Florida and Texas, as well as many other states. Lobbyists chummy with lawmakers protected not the dwindling fish,

Fishermen remember too well how commercial gill nets depleted fish stocks badly in coastal waters of Florida and Texas.

but profiteers. Fish populations plummeted.

Nowhere was the commercial overkill so egregious as in Florida. It took rank-and-file citizens, mostly anglers, to stop it.

After the legislature and management bodies failed year after year to tame the entangling nets, *Florida Sportsman* in 1991 initiated a campaign to get rid of the gill nets through a constitutional amendment by the people.

The plea for action hit a responsive note. Working with the Florida Conservation Association (now the Coastal Conservation Association Florida), a Save Our Sealife Coalition was formed. A commercial lobbyist promptly called it the "Mother of All Fish Wars."

The campaign required 429,428 validated petitions to force the issue to the ballot. Anglers collected those petitions without a single payment to petition gatherers, an unprecedented achievement. "People had fires in their bellies and worked day and night to get the job done," observed one leader.

Finally, after two years of verbal warfare and sometimes bizarre happenings, the proposed amendment went to the voters in November 1994. The amendment called for prohibiting all gill/entanglement nets and limiting inshore seine-type gear to 500 square feet.

This commercial rollernet boat, part of a fleet, took millions of pounds of Spanish mackerel. Today they use smaller castnets for the harvest.

Only a few years ago, it was legal to purse seine millions of pounds of large redfish. That practice has been stopped.

Yes, said the voters, overwhelmingly. It was a landslide 72 percent victory. The Net Ban, as it's called because of its complete gill net pro-

Saving the fish for tomorrow and the next generation of fishermen is a sacred trust.

hibition, took effect July 1, 1995.

Fish came back fast. The citizen initiative has been called the most revolutionary fisheries reform of modern times, considering the large size of the embedded commercial industry in Florida and the resounding effects of the change.

Stocks of crucial forage fish, notably mullet, soared threefold and more, benefiting not only gamefish but ospreys, turtles, pelicans, porpoises and other marine life. Seatrout exploded in numbers, leading to far greater catches as well as a much larger biomass in the wild. Pompano populations grew so quickly that many anglers learned to catch them for the first time. It's been the same nearly everywhere in Florida.

Some state officials have tried to minimize effects of the net ban, being somewhat embarrassed, understandably, since they hadn't taken any action themselves against gill nets, and many state staffers were cozy with the commercial industry for years. But the typical Florida angler saw, and is still seeing, the net ban improvements first-hand, praising the reform as changing their fisheries forever.

All kinds of loophole attempts and outright illegal netting undermined the amendment's effect to a small overall extent, and the battles continue. Overall, the momentum for change seems assured, at least on many state levels.

Commercial conflicts of interest still wrongly influence federal management, but even this is likely to change gradually.

Reforms have hardly been limited to Florida.

The state of Texas de-commercialized redfish and trout way back in 1981 and banned gill nets seven years later. Again, anglers were key to the conservation efforts, working with state officials who in Texas were sensitive to individual citizens rather than market forces.

Louisiana reacted to Florida's reform by banning most gill nets there as well.

One of the nation's premier coastal species,

the striped bass, also has made a spectacular comeback in many northern regions because of stricter regulations and de-commercializations at the behest of you, the angler. Organizations like the Coastal Conservation Association and Stripers Forever make the difference. If you're not already aboard the conservation train, there's a seat waiting for you.

We do oppose by the way, total-no-take marine reserves that ban family-level fishing, even when it has nothing to do with a depletion.

Wise-use conservation, rather than lockouts of personal fishing in ill-advised reserves, is the right goal.

A separate component of good conservation is care of the habitat, cleaning up our waters and keeping them healthy.

The striped bass has also made a good comeback, thanks to good conservation.

Here again, anglers often have been the citizens coming to the rescue. A prime and historic example was a group of recreational fishermen who blew the whistle on horrendous but ignored industrial pollution in the great Hudson River in New York.

All across America, sadly, our rivers once were treated as convenient sewers. Those waterways now have been transformed to a large extent, often because of demands of outdoor sport-related interests.

Agricultural and urban runoffs still spew excessive nutrients into our waters, however, and the fight is far from won or done. That's where you're really needed.

Meanwhile, nothing will enhance management of our existing fisheries more than for us to insist that all citizens be treated equally. Let's have no catches by the ton, please. We should practice sound conservation ourselves in every way possible.

Unfortunately, a large num-ber of fishermen want nothing to do with the politics of habitat protection and fishing regulations. We often pay a dear price for this apathy.

Even so, relatively small numbers of dedicated folks can make crucial differences.

We hope you'll be one of them. SB

Hatcheries Help Out

State coastal hatcheries have been successful at boosting coastal populations of some fish. Redfish fingerlings like those below have been grown and released into Texas bays by the tens of milions, with an upsurge in catch rates. Striped bass have also been raised and released by the U.S. Fish and Wildlife Service for a long time. It takes funding, land for the ponds and a paid staff to pull it off, but it certainly does work. About an inch long, these fingerlings are quick to swim away when released from the hatchery truck. They find a new home in shallow, protected backwaters with time to grow. SB

Fishing in Other Countries

Many anglers are dialed in on the amazing shallow water fishing in the Caribbean, as well as Central and South America. While there you don't have to pay for guide fees every day, to find good scenery and action. If you pack your own two-piece rods in a small tube, with reels and small tacklebox, even more options open up. This particular spot was reached by taxi on Long Island, Bahamas, on a day when the wind blew a steady 25 knots. No other fishermen were sighted the entire day.

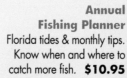

INSHORE FISHING DVD

Sportsman's Best: Inshore Fishing DVD brings the written pages of this book to life. The editors and publisher of Florida Sportsman and Shallow Water Angler magazines travel from Texas to New England, fishing with some of the best inshore experts out there, to bring you the most informative, comprehensive and exciting DVD ever produced on inshore saltwater fishing.

FEATURES
- **THE APPEAL OF INSHORE FISHING**
- **THE GAME PLAN**
- **TACKLE OPTIONS**
  - The Whole Arsenal
- **FAVORITE SPECIES**
- **WHAT'S AVAILABLE FROM BOAT OR SHORE**
  - Stealthy Wading
  - Structure
  - The Stakeout
- **TECHNIQUES**
  - Topwater Thrills
  - The Art of Jigging
  - Live Bait
  - The Water Column
- **FISHING STRATEGIES**
  - Tide Secrets
  - Reading the Water
  - Stealthy Shallows
  - **SAFETY**

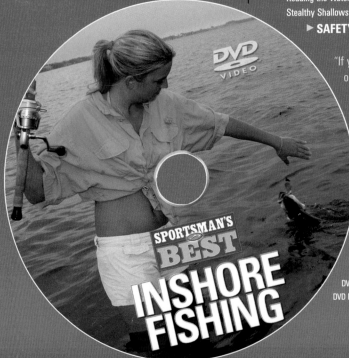

"If you're a shallow water angler or want to become one, this DVD is for you. It covers all the bases, fishing in at least five different states, with ten different guides and the hosts and editors of Shallow Water Angler and Florida Sportsman—you couldn't get more information in 60 minutes."

Publisher, Blair Wickstrom

DVD Executive Producer: Paul Farnsworth
DVD Production Assistant: Matt Weinhaus